A Child Is a Poem You Learn by Heart

by

Paulette Whitehurst

Cover art by Dane at ebooklaunch.com.

Author's Note

All the events and experiences here are factual and represented faithfully according to my memories and those memories my mother related to me. Although this is a work of nonfiction, some names have been changed and some characters have been written into composites in order to protect the privacy of those involved.

FAIRY FORT BOOKS, LLC
Chesterfield, VA

ISBN 978-0-578-70178-3

For Clay, Emma, and Jack,
my grandchildren

For my children, Chris and Betsey.
I love you, and now you know
the rest of the story.

Loneliness and the feeling of being unwanted
is the greatest poverty.

Mother Teresa

A Child is a Poem

A child is a newborn idea
that drifts into your life
like the aroma of a fresh-baked pie,
filling a void
you never knew existed,
consuming your life
in ways you never wanted,
needing your creativity
in ways you never expected.

A child is
a muddle of thoughts
that boggles your mind like a familiar tune
you never possessed
and cannot keep within your grasp,
interrupting your sleep
for just the right lines,
draining your strength and inner wisdom,
revealing your soul
for the world to inspect.

A child is a poem you learn by heart,
someone you love
because she's yours,
crafted through your novice trials,
a gift you give to all the world.
A child is a poem you learn by heart.

Anderson, South Carolina, 1948

Taking the Baby

When Mama could no longer
bear the beatings
and the days in the bedroom,
she went to Aunt Wreatha's house
in South Carolina,
where she remained
for several months.

One Sunday after church,
John Henry stepped into the kitchen,
nodded to all the relatives.
          "I want to talk to you outside,"
          he said to my mama.

They stepped onto the back porch
while the relatives continued
to pass the plates of food
around the table.
I watched from my highchair
gnawing on a biscuit.
          "You're gonna come with me
          to the sheriff's office."
          He spit the words at my mama.
          "You are gonna take back that warrant
          against me."

Trembling, Mama said,
"No, John Henry.
I'm not going to do that."
She looked to the relatives for help.
John Henry grabbed her wrist,
squeezed her with
his strong fist. When his eyes
fell upon her stomach,
he paused.

    "Goddamn you, Onelia," he laughed,
    "I've got you right where I want you."

He stepped into the kitchen
and swooped me from the highchair
while the surprised relatives watched.

Mama chased after him as he
deposited me in the front seat
between him   and the cab driver.

My grandfather hurried to the bedroom,
unlocked a drawer to retrieve his .38,
a nickel-plated revolver, and then
stumbled out the front door
while inside the relatives continued
to pass the plates of food, take another
helping of succotash,
just one more bite of mashed potatoes.

My grandfather pulled the gun from his pocket.
"Come on now, Mr. Wilson,"
John Henry said, "You don't want to do that."

The cab driver leaned back
as my mama stretched over him
through the driver's window
to pull me close to her.

Then Mama and my grandfather
entered the kitchen,
looked at the relatives still eating.
Aunt Wreatha asked,
"Anyone want sweet potato pie?"

Mama's Boy

Mama returned to Virginia with my grandfather
(who I called Papa).
A few weeks later Aunt Jenny drove her
to the steps of the hospital
and left her there alone
although Mama was at only seven months
of her pregnancy,

Her baby boy was born
but taken away quickly by the nurses.
When she asked to see him
the nurses said, "The doctor
will be in to see you soon."
But the doctor didn't come.

The next day,
she called my grandfather
and said, "I got me a boy, Daddy."
But she was still unable to see
her baby boy.

On the third day,
Marie, her older sister,
came to get Mama
and Mama said,
"Marie, they won't let me see my baby."

"Your baby is dead.
Now let's go. I have to get to work."
Just like that.

    Your baby is dead.

Like saying somebody
burned the biscuits.

No one asked Mama what she
wanted to name her baby boy.
Aunt Marie named him James Clyde
after my uncle and my grandfather.

At home, Aunt Jenny told Mama
"Your baby wasn't right."
Mama cried and denied her words.

Then she went to the telephone booth
on the corner, her voice quivering
in that small space,
resting her head against the glass,
gasping between sobs.

The nurse told Mama,
"You had a beautiful baby, Onelia.
He just didn't have time to develop.
His lungs weren't strong enough."

Mama brought flowers to the cemetery.
She cried and held me close to her
as she grieved the baby boy
she never saw,
      never held,
          never even had the chance
              to give him his name.

Wallahalla, South Carolina, 1929
Mama's Sisters

Mama said Grandma Iva died
of childbed fever
only a day after delivering
Mama's stillborn sibling.

Grandma Iva's body
was worn out from bearing
six children in twelve years.
Or maybe she just died of
a broken heart
knowing her baby was dead.

Mama could not remember
a time when her sisters were nice to her.
She was not sure why.
Maybe because she was the baby,
and they resented looking after her
when their mother died?

Maybe girls with no mother
had a hard-enough time
looking after themselves
and didn't know how
to look after
someone
else.

Wallahalla, South Carolina, 1929
The Photograph

Morning came as sure as
bill collectors on payday.
Five little girls assembled
in the morning mist.

Papa's strong hands, weathered
by the South Carolina sun,
guided his girls to the spot bathed by the light.
Hungry chickens joined them,
unaware of the solemn occasion.

A borrowed camera captured their family
in that moment before Reverend Mitchell
carried the girls away in his Model-T Ford
to an orphanage in Georgia
where they would remain
for two years.

Girls in cotton shifts, their hair bobbed
for convenience of care,
Mama and my Aunt Jenny
clutched their dolls.
Aunt Marie, the second daughter,
held her hands in a prayerful pose,
while Aunt Wretha, the oldest,
held on to the two youngest, Mama
and my Aunt Audrey, as if she were accustomed

to that role. Papa, barely thirty,
closed his eyes
as the camera shutter snapped,
perhaps in a silent prayer.
It was a memory Papa would press
under glass like Queen Anne's lace,
a memory that would fade over the years
like the edges of the photograph.

Rhody Mae

When Mama was four years old
and her oldest sister was just twelve,
Papa married Rhody Mae, a sixteen-year-old,
and he brought his girls home
from the orphanage, smiling and saying,
"Girls, this here's your new mama."

When Papa went out to work in the fields,
Mama hugged Rhody Mae around her legs
and said, "I love you, Mama."
Rhody Mae slapped her away
and said,
"I ain't your mama,
and don't you ever forget it."

And Mama

            never

            forgot.

Anderson, South Carolina, 1944

The Hired Hand

Strung out from the back porch
to the oak tree in the yard,
the clothesline   with the weigh
                    dipped
of its burden.

John Henry watched sixteen-year-old Onelia
from the field
as she wrung out a shirt with her
strong hands. Arms sturdy from cutting
and hauling firewood, she stretched
and twisted,   r e a c h i n g
for the wet laundry,
w r i n g i n g   the water
from each piece by hand
And   p i n n i n g   it to the clothesline,
never aware of John Henry
          w a t c h i n g   her.

Her hand-me-down dungarees,
and a close-fitting red-checkered blouse
covered her well-developed curves,
her bare feet rusty red
from the summer dust.
A soft, brown wisp
fell from the clasp holding
her hair back from her face

revealing her best feature,
large deep-blue eyes.
An old farm truck pulled into the driveway,
kicked up dust beneath the wheels.
She dropped the shirt in her hand
running more like a softball player
than a graceful deer.
"Daddy! You're home!"
Papa smiled as he hugged his girl.

John Henry watched her long legs
and her youthful features
until the field boss's hand on his shoulder
reminded him it was time
to get back to work.

Anderson, South Carolina, 1944

Sharecropping Life

Mama dropped out
of high school
and went to work at Woolworth's
even though she won the award
for the best Home Economics student
and Mrs. Jones, her math teacher,
said Mama had a real good head for figures.

John Henry joined the army,
sent Mama love letters
from faraway places
she had never heard of.
He went AWOL to visit her.
She fell in love with his uniform
and the idea of being married
like her sisters.

With her sisters grown
and Papa working on an Army base in Louisiana,
Rhody Mae rented a farm where
she taught Mama to cook and
clean, sew, can vegetables,
make jellies, jams, and pickles.

Rhody Mae took her to church and taught
her to fear the Lord.

Mama and Rhody Mae
cried together when they
heard on the radio
that President Roosevelt died.

Anderson, South Carolina, 1945
Newlyweds

John Henry wanted to marry Mama, and
Rhody Mae thought it was a good idea.
Papa was still working in Louisiana.
They would live with Rhody-Mae
and help her with the farm.
Mama had met John Henry's family in Georgia, and
she loved them as much as they loved her.

Mama put a navy-blue suit and
a pair of matching shoes on layaway.
Rhody Mae planned the event
which took place in her living room.

She fixed the wedding dinner and
sent them off to bed in Mama's bedroom.
When morning came,
Mama told John Henry
she didn't want to be married
anymore.

John Henry never hit Mama during
their courtship. He showed her the attention
she craved, and she just wanted to be married,
like her sisters.

But after their marriage,
he hit her often and the hitting
escalated to beatings.

At first she was stunned.
No one had ever treated her this way.
After many months of beatings,
bruised and crying, Mama told
Rhody Mae she wanted out,
but Rhody Mae said,
"You made your bed,"
then she added
"and now you gotta lie in it."

And John Henry said,
"Shut up. You're my wife, and
you're gonna do what I say,
Goddamn ya."

John Henry took Mama
and moved to Georgia
to live with his family.

Lavonia, Georgia, 1945

The Decision

In Georgia, the beatings continued.
He not only beat Mama, he beat
his younger brothers and sisters,
and no one stopped him.

Mama decided
to leave John Henry
the night she hid in that Georgia ditch
as rain pelted her body
until her cotton house dress
clung to her skin.

Rain so steady, the hard, red Georgia clay
loosened and formed
small rivers that spilled
into puddles.

Except for the uncontrollable chattering
of her teeth, she crouched silently,
head down in the tall grass,
as John Henry trampled
through the puddles,
searching.

His voice exploded above the storm:
"I know you're out there
and sooner or later,
I'm gonna whoop your ass."

Mama told herself she would go
to Virginia to join her two of her sisters,
and she was never coming back.

That's what
she told herself.

Freeloading

When Papa left Louisiana
and started working in Virginia,
Mama left Georgia and traveled
to Portsmouth, Virginia
to live with Papa and
her two married sisters, Jenny and Marie.

The sisters resented her,
called her a freeloader,
but Papa took up for her.
The sisters told her to go
back to Georgia and stay
with her husband.

Mama's sisters liked John Henry
because he smiled at them
and told them how
pretty they looked.
They blamed Mama
for her marriage problems.

Aunt Marie told Mama that
John Henry was a good man.
If she would just behave herself
like a good wife,
everything would be fine.

When John Henry showed up
in Portsmouth
and wanted Mama back,
Papa said he would help him
get a job and then reminded Mama
that their Church of God religion
did not approve of divorce.

Jealous Rage

Mama and John Henry
moved into an upstairs room
in a little house
beside the railroad tracks.
The landlady gave them
use of her kitchen.

Papa helped John Henry get a job
at the bus garage next door.
John Henry thought this
a convenience so he
could come home at any time
to demand sex.

One morning, Mama had planned
to go shopping with Aunt Marie,
but John Henry told her she could not go.
He liked having her in the house
where he could control who she saw,
who she talked with,
what she did.

That morning he hid Mama's
partial plate, knowing she
would not leave the house
without her teeth, but Mama
called Papa for help.

Papa came, stomped across the porch,
and banged on the door.

When Mama opened the door,
Papa entered and demanded,
"John Henry, give her those teeth right now.
They belong to her. I paid for them.
And don't you ever take them again!"

John Henry laughed,
"Come on, Mr. Wilson,
I was just kidding around."

She left with Aunt Marie
knowing that she would
probably get a beating
when she returned, but
later that evening,
when Mama returned,
immediately she called
Papa and Aunt Marie
on the phone and said,
"Come over here right now.
You have got to see this to believe it.
You ain't never seen nothin' like this
in your whole life."

John Henry had been in the pantry
and cut open all the cans,
ripped open the bags of sugar and flour,
and everything

was in the middle
of the kitchen floor.
Upstairs, he took her clothes
and cut them to ribbons.

Papa said he was gonna
have him arrested
and Mama was gonna
swear that he hit her again,
but John Henry had gone
and left town,
took his paycheck,
and all the money he had saved.
There was nothing she could do.

Papa and Aunt Marie told her
she had to go back to him because
Mama was going to have his baby—
        me.
But Mama refused, saying
she was tired of the beatings
and could not take it anymore.

Then they left Mama there
to clean up the mess alone.
She picked up the corn and the beans
from the kitchen floor,
swept up the flour and the sugar,
along with her hope
that this marriage would work out.

The Apology

Living with Aunt Marie,
Mama took care of Marie's children,
cleaned her house,
scrubbed the floors and wore
Marie's hand-me-down dresses.

Mama wanted to work and
earn her own money,
buy her own dresses,
but she was stuck watching Marie's
babies, and Mama—with another baby
in her belly.

A letter came in the mail
apologizing for John Henry's
behavior, promising he would not
behave as he had done before,
never again.

The only problem was that
the letter was from his mother.
The apology was from
my Granny.

Portsmouth, Virginia, 1946
She Wanted More

Mama never wanted anything
in her whole life
except to be a wife and a mother.
She wanted so much for this
marriage to work out.
She loved John Henry's family,
and they loved her:
one of the reasons she agreed
to marry him.
And he was so handsome in
that Army uniform.

Papa said, "Let him come back
and I'll find him a job."
She agreed to try again although
her heart was heavy with doubt.
John Henry came back,
and they moved in with Papa.

When Papa went to work
John Henry beat Mama badly
and forced her to have sex
although she was close to
her delivery date, and she
begged him not to.

Then, he left and told her he was never

                              coming

                                          back.

Mama thought that all she
wanted was to be a wife
and a mother, but
now she realized,
                    she wanted more.

Christmas Eve Baby

On the night I was born
Aunt Jenny drove Mama to the
hospital and let her out in front
before driving away
to avoid financial responsibility
All alone, delirious
from the pain
and her shattered illusions,
Mama wished herself dead.
A nurse slapped her
for what she had said,
and a welfare doctor
stood over my mama
at the delivery table
wrenching me
from her warm body, and
placing me in the nursery
alongside a baby girl
named Noel.

In the maternity ward
chenille-robed mothers
browsed the pages
of Dr. Spock,
bestowed smiles
from their flowered thrones

and accepted gifts
with practiced ease
like contestants on
Queen for a Day.

Behind the curtain,
my mother's tears
saturated her pillowcase
and spotted her hospital-green gown.
But the next day,
maybe because she believed in fairy tales,
or perhaps because
she wanted to give me
the gift of glamour,
she borrowed my name,
Paulette Lucille,
from two smiling movie stars
in a worn copy
of a *Photoplay* magazine.

Papa's House

After my birth, Mama brought me home
to my grandfather's house,
where the air was saturated
with cigar smoke and country music.
Papa was the first man in my life.
Mama said he was a proud grandfather
who fed me the juice of honeydew
melons from his coffee spoon
when I was only six weeks old.

Mama's sisters came to visit us,
but they always made Mama cry.
Mama said they blamed her
for John Henry's behavior.
They blamed her for the beatings.
If she were just a better wife,
he wouldn't beat her.
They wanted her to return to
John Henry and be a good wife.

Papa just shook his head and walked
away with slumped shoulders as the
sisters fussed.

Lavonia, Georgia, 1947
Return to Georgia

Mama gave in to her sisters'
relentless demands that she return
to her husband.
She packed her suitcase,
     put aside her apprehensions,
          and bundled me in warm blankets
for our bus trip.

All the Georgia relatives were happy
to see Mama and to hold the baby.
John Henry, who had beaten Mama
only a few months before,
hugged her and took her into the bedroom,
where he kept her
for three days except for occasional
trips to the outhouse.

Mama didn't scream.
She was embarrassed and
wondered why the others
didn't interfere,
and John Henry reminded her
"Shut up. You're my wife, and
you're gonna do what I say,
Goddamn ya."

Portsmouth, Virginia, 1948

Mama's Decision

After her baby boy died,
and that close call when John Henry
tried to take me away that Sunday
at Aunt Wreatha's house,
Mama told my grandfather:
"I'm not going back to Georgia, and
I'm not going back to South Carolina—
not anymore."

She pulled a cigarette from her package
of Kools and lit it, knowing that her father
disapproved of her new habit.
"I'm going to get a job.
I can take care of myself and Paulette."
Papa nodded in resignation.

That's when Mama found two jobs,
and placed an ad in the newspaper
to find a place for me to stay.

Portsmouth, Virginia, 1948
The Ghost of Toni

When I was eighteen months of age
Mama lifted me into her arms
and delivered me to the home
of Joe and Louise.

They were strangers, an Italian couple
with good manners who answered
Mama's ad in the newspapers.
Nice people with a clean house,
a house devoid of children
except for the ghost of Toni,
whose life was snatched
by leukemia when she
was seven years old.

Although I folded my rosebud
nightgown and tucked it under
her pillow, and I sat in her chair
at the breakfast table,
I could never be Toni.

Toni, whose name was always
whispered like a solemn prayer.
Toni, whose dolls were never
to be touched.
Toni, who always brushed her teeth
without being reminded.

Toni, who brushed her hair 100 strokes
before bedtime every night.
Toni, who always picked up her toys
and never disobeyed,
Toni, who always ate everything
on her plate because children in
China were starving.

Wherever I went in that house
Toni smiled down on me:
from the piano top, the mantel board
over the fireplace, the bedroom
dresser.

Toni reminded me to eat
everything on my plate
even the rubbery mushrooms
that gagged me because they were
as big as my hands.

Just chew and swallow.

Ti Amo, Joe

Sometimes Louise took me shopping,
and we stopped to see Joe at work
in his barbershop:
Joe, with his slicked-back hair,
straight and shiny,
was always happy to see me.

Joe smelled like Old Spice shaving lotion,
and laughed out loud when he saw me.
He rode me up and down in his barbershop chair.

Joe laughed with me at home
when we listened to *Amos and Andy* on the radio.
I had no idea what was so funny, but
it felt so good to laugh. I didn't
want it to stop

Joe purchased a television set and
watched *Howdy Doody* with me.
When I wanted to wear my hair in braids
like Princess Summerfall Winterspring
Louise agreed, but when I said that
I wanted to look like the Indian princess
when I grew up,
Louise laughed and said
that would never happen.

One day, Joe came home from work
with a doll for me. I named her Susie.
Susie had long eyelashes, big blue eyes
that blinked, and a sweet smile on her lips.

After that day, Susie was always by my side.
When Joe tucked me into bed at night,
and heard my prayers, he kissed me
and Susie goodnight,
but he never left my bedside
before saying,
"Ti amo."

Shoe Shopping

Louise took me
to Hofheimer's Shoe Store
on High Street.
Shoes of all shapes and sizes
filled the store window.
Inside the store
the boxes stacked on shelves
reached the ceiling.
Salesmen climbed ladders
to find another size, another color.

High heels for fancy ladies,
and pocketbooks to match,
boots for big working men,
and Buster Brown shoes
for little people like me.

I raced to the back of the store
where the caged monkey chattered
behind the glass.
I giggled and made faces at him
until Louise pulled me away saying,
"Get away from that nasty creature!"

Within a few minutes
I was wearing my new
black patent leather Mary Janes,
and looking at my toes

through a viewer in the
shoe-fitting flouroscope machine
while other children stood
in line behind me
to wiggle their toes
on the X-ray just for fun.

Portsmouth, Virginia, 1951
Visiting Days

When Mama came to visit,
I watched her approach from
the bus stop,
recognizing her slumped shoulders,
her tired gait,
even before I saw her face.
Tired from the top of her
pin-curled hair
to the soles of her white
waitress shoes.

I danced on tippy-toes
across the neighbor's yard
to meet her.
She was beautiful with her shiny hair,
her dark red lips, and her rouged cheeks.

The times I liked best
were when Mama had a friend
who drove her in a car
to pick me up, and we
left Louise's watchful
eyes to visit alone.

But we had to return,
and then I cried, knowing
that the time would be long
until I would see her again.

Portsmouth, Virginia, 1951
The Woods

Sometimes on Mama's day off
she took me to visit my cousins.
Running, screaming, hiding,
seeking, laughing, playing,
imagining, in the woods,
a little patch of trees
on Cavalier Boulevard.

It was never too cold,
too hot, or too wet.
Splashing
in the little ditch
we called a stream,
we spent hours,
building forts and
shooting our cap guns,
playing hide-and-seek,
head against a tree counting
with my eyes closed
and peeking to see
where everyone hid.

TAG!
You're it!

Portsmouth, Virginia, 1951
Penny Candy

On the best of days
my cousins and I each had a dime
for penny candy
and followed the path
to Rose's 5 & 10
to spend it.

I put my dime on the top
of the glass counter
and began the difficult process
of choosing from the delicious
array of penny candy.
Mary Janes, B-B bats,
bubblegum, jawbreakers,
Tootsie Pops.
I glanced up at the saleslady,
bleached blonde curls
escaping from her blue bandana,
a cigarette with long ashes drooping
precariously from her dark red lips.
"Hurry up, kid. I got things to do."

She had my little brown bag open
and ready to drop in my treats.
I pointed to the Tootsie Rolls
knowing they were two for a penny.
I pointed to the jawbreaker
knowing that it would last for a long time.

I chose a chewy Mary Jane—
and then the wax lips to make Mama laugh.

I pointed to the candy cigarettes.
She reached for the Lucky Strikes.
"No, not that one—the Kools," I said,
"so I can look like Mama."

Portsmouth, Virginia, 1952
Irwin's Pharmacy

All the customers
loved Mama, and they smiled at me
when I came to work with her.

In the window at Irwin's Pharmacy
among the red and green paper
decorations and the boxed dolls
covered with cellophane,
I saw my photo.
Red pleated skirt and
creamy white sweater,
my black patent leather shoes
and clean white socks.
My pearls, my curls,
and the satin bow in my hair.
Holding a book in my hands,
a book with magnificent sailboats
floating across a turquoise sea.

That was me in the photograph,
the one in the window
of Irwin's Pharmacy
where Mama worked.
A note in the window read,
"Onelia's girl."

Portsmouth, Virginia, 1952

Tips and Turns

I loved my booth in the back
of Irwin's Pharmacy
with its red plastic
seats and silvery grey
Formica tabletop.
I saw everything from there.

I chose the perfect shade of blue
from my crayon box
for the bridesmaids' dresses
in my coloring book.

I watched Mama and the other waitresses
in their cotton-candy-pink uniforms and
white ruffled aprons
as they tended to their customers
at the lunch counter as carefully as
Louise tended to her African violets.

I watched the men flirt and the waitresses
smile and collect their tips.
On the shelf above me, the silver
tinsel Christmas tree rotated
and changed from red to blue
to green.

Portsmouth, Virginia, 1952
The Parade

When Mama got off work,
she took me outside to see
the Christmas parade
right in front of Irwin's Pharmacy.
We watched from the corner of
Crawford and High Streets,
moving to the music
of the marching high school bands
with their jazzed-up Christmas songs.

We waved to the local
officials as they passed in cars.
I strained to see between
the legs of the spectators until
Mama placed me right
in front of her.

Smiling ladies in fur coats and
sparkling dresses drove by
in shiny cars without tops,
waved their long-gloved arms,
adjusted the crowns that topped
their stylish hairdos.

Military groups passed,
Army, Marines, some marching,
some being pushed in wheelchairs
or riding in cars.

Mama leaned over to explain to me
that some of them had war injuries.

The Navy band played "Anchors Aweigh"
as sailors marched by
in their dress uniforms
with our nation's flag held high.

The crowds cheered and whistled
as they passed, and Mama explained
that Portsmouth was a Navy town.
I placed my hand on my heart
like Mama, as I bounced
with the rhythm of the Navy fight song.

The silly clowns skipped along
with their big red noses
and their oversized shoes
and threw peppermint candies
to the little kids
who scrambled to
retrieve their treats

"Oh, boy!" Mama said,
"Here comes Cradock High School!
They are the best!"

I heard their drumbeats
long before they appeared.
Majorettes dressed in maroon and gold
carried their school's banner

and beamed with pride,
the brass instruments bounced
to and fro with the rhythm of the music.

Out in front of the band
a beautiful majorette,
twirled her baton
and threw it high into the air—
catching it as it fell.
The crowd applauded.
A lady followed
alongside the band,
pointing and screaming,
"That's my baby! That's my baby!"
This made the crowd laugh,
and Mama told me,
"That must be her daughter.
She is proud of her girl."

The beautiful majorette lifted
her head back, smiling, and stepped
even higher as the crowd applauded.

> *She is proud of her girl.*

I watched them as they continued
marching down High Street
even after they passed
the courthouse steps where the
old men of Portsmouth gathered
every day on the park benches

to smoke their cigars and
swap their stories.

I wanted to do something
one day to make
my Mama proud.

Portsmouth, VA, 1952
Now I Am Six

Rapt in the glow
of Christmas tree lights
and birthday candles,
I posed for the camera
clothed in green velvet and lace.
Showing off my curls
from the Tonette home
permanent that Louise gave me
at the kitchen table.

Now I am six,
and with wrist extended,
I displayed my Cinderella watch
and my Shirley Temple smile.

Mama promised she would
take me to live with her when
I turned six
and could go to school.

And now I am six.

Portsmouth, Virginia, 1953
Mama Takes Me with Her

On a gray January day
Mama arrived with an
empty suitcase.
From my bedroom,
I heard their voices
in the kitchen,
charged with emotion
"I come to get my girl."

I stuffed my Howdy Doody
puppet and a box of colored chalk
in Mama's suitcase.

Louise picked up the receiver
of the black telephone
in the living room
and dialed,
but not even a talk
with Joe dissuaded Mama.
She wanted her girl.

Mama and Louise both cried.
Louise pleaded with her
and talked of adoption.
Mama startled me when
she slammed her fist
on the tabletop.

Louise buttoned my camel coat
and smoothed my hair
before tying on my matching cap.
When we pulled out of the driveway
I saw Louise tugging at her cotton apron
before offering a little wave
from the back-porch stoop.

I smiled at her through the
back window of the car and waved
as I whispered,

                    "No more mushrooms."

Portsmouth, Virginia, 1953

Mr. Murphy

Mama married Mr. Murphy
and we moved to an upstairs apartment
on Washington Street overlooking
the funeral home next door.

Soon Mr. Murphy stole a car,
drove it to Kansas to see his family,
and returned to Virginia, where he parked
the stolen car on a side street
not in front of our apartment.
But it made no difference.
He was caught anyway.

He was surprised
when the police came to get him.
He was kicked out of the Navy
and spent some time in jail,
where Mama took me to visit
my new daddy.

Portsmouth, Virginia, 1953
Children Should Be Seen and Not Heard

When I moved in with Mama
and Mr. Murphy,
I missed my bicycle
and my pigtails with satin ribbons,
but I didn't miss Louise.
I was with Mama all the time now.
No more visiting days.

Mama walked me to school and took me
to visit Joe at his barbershop just around
the corner from our apartment.

Mr. Murphy said we were moving, and
he told Mama not to take me to see
that dago barber again.

Mr. Murphy wore a white sailor suit
and smelled of cigarettes. He never smiled.
Mr. Murphy smirked,
"Children are to be seen and not heard."
Mama tried to make me like him,
but I never did.

Mr. Murphy took me out of the bathtub
and sat me on the oil stove in the living room
causing a painful burn on my bottom.

But Mama said it was okay because he said,
"sorry."

And when Mr. Murphy painted my bedroom,
I decorated the walls with all 64 colors
in my crayon box, and
I screamed but refused to cry
when he hit me with his belt,
and I would not say, "sorry."

Hickory, Virginia
Summer, 1953

Living in the Sticks

Mr. Murphy moved us to a
little house in the country where bats
came inside at night and flapped around
if you left the windows open.

He bought a television set so
he could watch the fights at night.
He began adjusting the television
before the show came on,
playing around with the rabbit ears
until he had the best reception he
could get for living in the sticks.

When the show came on,
he raised his beer can and sang
along with the little cartoon people
as they bounced around the screen,
"You'll look sharp and feel sharp, too..."

He balled up his fists and waved
his arms around imagining himself
in the ring. He cussed at the screen
whenever he disagreed
with the referee's decisions, until
Mama said, "Shhh. Little pitchers
have big ears."

When Mr. Murphy went to work,
Mama watched her soap operas
and game shows, and every afternoon
the neighborhood children
gathered at 5:30 to watch *Howdy Doody* with me.

Mama said that was okay
as long as they left before
Mr. Murphy came home.

Deep Creek Elementary School

I went to my second school in first
grade and rode a bus
instead of walking with Mama.
But my new school would not allow me
to enter second grade with only
one semester of first grade behind me.
I thought the children were babies,
because they could not read like me
but the best thing about my new school
was that the teacher allowed me
to take my book home
to read.

I loved Dick and Jane, Sally, Puff, and Spot.
Their adventures with spilled milk,
water hoses, and chocolate cakes
made me laugh. And I smiled as
I read the book
to my mama.

On the Road,
October, 1953

Family Adventure

Mama announced to
friends and family that
a wife has to follow
where her husband leads.
And the more she explained
the more she convinced herself.

"We will see new places,"
she said.
"We will meet new people,"
she said,
"It will be an adventure,"
she said.
"You have a new daddy now."

Mr. Murphy pulled his cigarettes
from his rolled-up shirt sleeve and said,
"Let's get going. We have a long ride
ahead of us."

Like pioneers on the cowboy shows
we watched on television,
we crept across the country
in an old Buick with Mr. Murphy,
my new daddy,
in the driver's seat
in search of a better life.

Sandwiched between the door
and the mountain of boxes
holding Mama's treasures,
I stowed away in the back seat
with my doll, Susie,
and a worn copy of
Fun with Dick and Jane
that I failed to return to school.

On the Road
October, Dayton, Ohio, 1953
Ohio Cousins

Mama told me all about my Ohio cousins.
Aunt Audrey wore a smile
and a blue calico dress. She hugged me
and squeezed Mama's hands,
fed us warm soup and homemade bread.
Aunt Audrey called Mama her
baby sister. I slept on the floor on a
pallet of blankets with a tangle of cousins.

On the lawn in front of their home,
Uncle Art lifted me and my cousins
under our arms and swung us around
in circles under the wide Ohio sky,
as Mr. Murphy watched.
We stumbled around, dizzy,
giggling as the world spun by.
On Halloween night we went door-to-door
gathering treats and then spread them out
on the living room floor to count.

Aunt Audrey begged us to stay,
but when she could see that
we wouldn't, she buttoned me

into an almost-new warm woolen coat,
slipped money into Mama's pocket,
and then wiped her eyes
as our old Buick sputtered off
down the road toward Indiana.

On the Road, 1953
Roadside Dreams

We crossed the Mississippi River
and pulled off the road
to sleep while sheets of rain
pounded against the roof of the Buick.

M – I – crooked letter - crooked letter – I -
crooked letter - crooked letter – I –
humpback – humpback - I.

I dreamed of a blue sky
and two strong arms
that lifted me to the powder puff
clouds, swinging me around.
I looked for Uncle Art's smile,
but I could not see him.

I heard my new daddy's voice:
"Children," he said,
"should be seen and not heard."

On the Road, 1953
Kansas

In Kansas, we visited Mr. Murphy's Mama.
Pulling the Buick into the barn,
Mr. Murphy said,
"Wait here," before slipping out the door and
heading for the house.

Mama said,
"He will be back soon." And we waited
like Mr. Murphy told us to do.

After a while, Mr. Murphy
returned with his mama, a small
lady with a stern weathered face.
"Come on inside for something to eat,"
she said. "And then you have to go.
I don't want no trouble."

On the Road, 1953
Mr. Murphy's Mama

The wind howled and whipped
up my coat as we approached
the old farmhouse, and I held Mama's hand
as we entered.

After Mr. Murphy's mama served us a bowl
of hot beans and cold biscuits,
she held her hands on her round tummy
rubbing them on her apron
as she watched us eat.

Mama tried to talk to Mr. Murphy's mama,
"It's right kind of you to—"
but Mr. Murphy interrupted,
"Just eat up and let's go. I should have known
better than to expect any help here."

Mr. Murphy's mama twisted her mouth
and pressed her lips together tightly.
"I done told ya, I don't want no trouble."

I heard someone call out from another part of the house.
Mr. Murphy jerked open the kitchen door and
motioned for us to get back to the barn.
Mr. Murphy's mama grabbed my hands
and shoved a cloth package to me.
We were soon back in the Buick and
headed down the highway again.

I opened the cloth and found
two more biscuits inside.
It was many years before Mama
would discover that Mr. Murphy
never divorced his first wife
and that was the reason for his
mother's reluctance to help us.

Denver, Colorado
November, 1953

Colorado Nights

Along a wide Denver highway
the motel sign
flashed VACANCY
and a neon cowboy atop
the office beckoned to us.
The tires crunched the snow
leaving marks in the driveway.

We entered our one-room cabin
where we found a green vinyl dinette set,
and a cement floor covered by
a linoleum rug with blue roses.
There was an ice box, but no ice,
but Mama said it was okay.
"We will just sit the milk
on the windowsill outside."

Covered with a lime-green
corduroy bedspread, the double bed
was a welcome sight.
Slipping off our clothing,
all three of us climbed into the bed
lying side-by-side like spoons
in Louise's silver chest.
Susie slept close by my side.

Icicles suspended from the roof outside
glistened in the Colorado moonlight as
the winter moon peeped
at us through pink plastic curtains.
On that cold Colorado night
wind rattled our door
and snowflakes kissed
the windowpanes.

I closed my eyes
to think of Virginia and
see my grandfather's smile,
hear the creak of the porch swing,
embrace the warmth
of the dappled sunlight
filtering through the protection
of the sycamore tree as it sprouted
out of the sidewalk cracks
and spread out over the house
like a Chinese fan.

Breathing deeply, I dreamed
of roasting peanuts wafting
from the Skippy factory nearby.
As I drifted off into sleep I thought
I heard the 10 o'clock train
whistle as it rumbled
past Papa's back door.

Denver, Colorado,
November, 1953

The Last Argument

Mr. Murphy looked for a job
every day and returned
to our motel room at night
with empty pockets
and a somber face.
Arguments were frequent
and noisy.

One night, Mr. Murphy pulled
his suitcase from under the bed
and began throwing in his clothing.

Mama sent me to the shower house
in the snowy courtyard,
but once outside,
I peeped through the window.

Mr. Murphy shouted,
"I can't help it. There's just
no work here for me."

Mama said, "Maybe you should have
thought of that before we drove
all this way! And if you think
I'm going to sit here and wait
for you while you go gallivanting
all over the place, you are sadly mistaken."

I watched
as he left with his suitcase,
slammed the cabin door,
and drove away.

Mama cried all through the night.
I rubbed her arm and
patted her back.
I told her everything
would be all right.

She whispered through
her tears: "I don't need him.
I don't need anybody."

Drugstore Job

Mama found work at a Walgreens drugstore
lunch counter where she soon met Danny,
a kind customer, who offered his friendship.

We settled into a routine: work for Mama,
school for me, (my third school in first grade),
and Danny, inching into our lives.
Our motel cabin felt more like home.

Colorado snow, wonderful, white, and powdery,
made up for some of the things
I missed in Virginia.
But it couldn't fix everything.

Danny took us for rides in his pink Cadillac,
into the mountains surrounding Denver.
We peered down on Monopoly-sized buildings
and cars. Danny and Mama laughed together,
and he called me "Little Lady."

Mr. Murphy faded from our thoughts and
conversation like the last snow of winter.
I wondered if Danny would be
my new daddy.

Christmas Dreams

A fresh snowfall
transformed the parking lot
into a fairyland of diamond dust
sparkling in the sunlight.
I held Susie, tightly
as we danced around
singing all the songs we knew.
"Oh, Susannah" and "Oh, Say Can You See,"
but Susie and I didn't know
all the words to that one.
Creating snow angels on our backs,
mine child-sized, Susie's, doll-sized,
we watched a hawk glide across
the clear blue sky, as I sang,
"Carry Me Back to Old Virginny."

I held Susie close to me and told her
that Santa would soon arrive
bringing us a tiny table and chairs
with little hearts painted on them
just like in our fairytale book.
Santa knew we wanted a china
tea set with delicate pink
roses for our elegant
tea parties, and a special

red plaid doll carriage for
Susie with a top to block out
the bright sunshine of hot summer days.
The anticipation was unbearable.

Can she bake a cherry pie, charming Billy?

Playing Games

Susie and I continued to play
in the motel courtyard every day after school:
knocking icicle soldiers
from the roof of the shower house,
peeking into car windows,
inventing stories about the owners
who were mostly overnight guests at the motel,
ladies pretty enough to be movie stars
but not as pretty as Mama.

Mama had long shiny hair
and big blue eyes
like Loretta Young on TV.
Mama could sing, too.
When I was a baby, Mama worked
in a restaurant in Atlanta.
A man heard her singing
and invited her
to go to New York with him.

Mama could have been a singer,
or a movie star if it had not been for me.
I was only a baby so Mama
could not go to New York.

Mama told me the story
many times.

One afternoon as I rested on a snowy swing
with Susie on my lap,
I assured her that Santa knew about
our long trip to Colorado
and how good we had been.
Surely, he would make
all our Christmas dreams come true.
I whispered to Susie about Danny,
about the way he smiled at Mama,
and about the way he held my hand
when we crossed the street.
I looked up and saw Mama
returning from work early.
I ran to greet her,
but when I saw her face
I knew that something
was wrong.

"Pack your suitcase!"
Mama insisted.
"What's wrong, Mama?"
I asked.

"We can only take what we can carry,"
she said. "We'll send for the rest later."

I trailed behind Mama
as we crossed the highway
to a telephone booth where Mama
made a tearful phone call to my grandfather
in Virginia.

As we climbed into a taxi for the ride
to the bus station, Danny drove
into the parking lot at the motel.
"Mama, it's Danny!" I squealed.
Mama just looked away with tears in her eyes.

Later I would learn that Mama
found out that day that Danny was married—
and Mama had no use for married men
who pretended
to be single.

On the Road Again, 1953
Riding the Greyhound

Nights and days melded
during the long hours
on the bus.

Quiet filled the musty
darkness. Now snores,
coughs, whispers
occupied the space filled
by lively conversations
during daylight.

I held Susie closely, comforting her
as I looked out the window,
made up stories, and sang
in whispered tones.

Oh, beautiful for spacious skies,
For amber waves of grain.

The Christmas tree lights
we longed to see were replaced
by the neon lights of the small towns
we saw from the bus window.

On the road again,
Christmas Eve, 1953
Happy Birthday to Me

Cold and sleepy,
Mama and I ran through the night
in a panic to catch our bus
when the driver pulled away early
from a bus stop diner in Missouri.

As the bus pulled out of the parking lot
I realized that I had left Susie behind.
I pressed my forehead against the bus window.
Tears streamed down my face
as I watched the diner fade
into the distance.

I imagined Susie sitting there
in the vinyl booth, abandoned,
smiling her sweet smile.
How would Santa ever find us now?

I drifted into a troubled sleep
cuddled against Mama's back,
vaguely aware of someone
crying softly during the long night.

Mama spent most of her time
sleeping or staring blankly
out the bus window.

When our bus passed a roadside
sign that proclaimed
"Welcome to Virginia,"
Mama's mood transformed,
her face reminiscent of
Susie's as she announced,
"We're almost home."

Portsmouth, Virginia, 1953
Virginia Dreams

My Virginia dreams were always the same.
Danny arrived in a pink Cadillac
about a mile long, Dean Martin
crooned *You Belong to Me* from the radio.

Susie sat beside Danny on the front seat.
Mama and I ran to meet them
through soft Colorado snow.
Mama's laughter filled the air.
Danny and Mama smiled at each other,
and I embraced Susie.

But my Virginia dreams never came true.
Santa never brought the table
with the little blue chairs or the china tea set.
And I still thought of Susie every Christmas
and wondered if she was sitting somewhere
smiling her sweet smile
in a red plaid carriage
with a top.

Portsmouth, Virginia
January, 1954

Changes

In the New Year, Papa moved
to his new house in Park View
and left us with his apartment on Queen Street.
Mama got her old job back at Irwin's Pharmacy
in the mornings, and she found a new job at night,
waitressing at a tavern called the Silver Slipper.

I stayed with our neighbor, Mrs. Harris,
While Mama worked nights.
She was a large lady with bright red hair.
Mrs. Harris's daughter, Judy,
became my big sister. I loved playing
with Judy when Mama worked.

I missed Papa playing with me,
sitting me on his lap to talk,
me riding on his leg like a horse,
but we would see him often.
The bus stopped right by his corner.

Sixth Avenue Elementary School

Mama took me to Sixth Avenue Elementary
where I attended
my fourth school in first grade.
When the principal, Mr. Music,
brought me into my new classroom,
he put papers on the teacher's desk,
turned quickly, and left me
in the care of Miss Wood.
She first frowned at me, then
turned to the class and said,
"Heads down."

I stood by her desk while she looked
over the papers Mr. Music had left with her.
Then she asked,
"What am I going to do with you?
I have too many children now!"

She began mumbling under her breath.
I wasn't sure if she expected
me to answer her.
"A child who has been in three different schools
already this year!"

My new classmates rested their heads
down on their desks and listened
as Miss Wood interrogated me.

"Why is your mother's last name
different from yours?"
she asked as she pointed to me
with her ruler.

"She married Mr. Murphy,"
I whispered,
"my stepfather."

"Humph," she raised her eyebrows
and her voice,
"What kind of mother
drags her child all over
the country
from school to school?"

"I don't know," I whispered.

"Go sit in the reading circle,"
she ordered,
"until I can get another chair in here.
I bet you can't even read."

I found my way over to the circle of little
chairs at the back of the classroom
and took a seat as I wondered,
"How long until summer?"

Portsmouth, Virginia, 1954

On My Own

Our neighbor, Mr. Harris,
slammed the screen door
on his way to work.
I awakened to sunlight
splashing across my bed.
I pushed back my scrap-quilt
and called out for Mama.
She was deep in sleep.
I stretched on tiptoe to pull my blue
cotton dress from a hanger in the closet.
Mama would be proud of me.
I would dress myself for school.
I pulled on my white bobby sox
and tied the laces
on my black and white
saddle shoes
before quietly closing
the apartment door and
walking the eight blocks
to school.

Portsmouth, Virginia, 1954
Late for School

The playground was empty.
The last line of single-file students
was shuffling through the doorway.
I approached the second-grade classroom
where they were already singing
"for spacious skies and amber waves of grain."
On tiptoe I peered through the glass
of the first-grade classroom.
Miss Wood was already in the reading
circle with the Bluebirds, her best readers.
Her black lace-up shoes tapped softly to
the rhythm of Sandy Harrigan's
impeccable performance.
I scooted into my seat
without a sound.
Buddy flashed me a toothless grin
from across the table.

Portsmouth, Virginia, 1954

What Kind of Bird Am I?

I clutched my fat school pencil between
my thumb and forefinger.
Perfect, bold strokes filled the page
and mirrored the chart at the
front of the class.
Up to the roof…down to the floor…
My big letters stood tall and strong
alongside the little ones.
The "S" stretched upward to kiss the blue line.
A "T" with arms outstretched offered
protection to the letters
on either side of him.
I strove for perfection to show Miss Wood
I am not a Blackbird.

Creamy tan hose with bulging ankles
appeared at my side.
In anticipation of praise,
I lifted my eyes to pursed lips
and squinty eyes
behind wire rims.
She took my arm
and pulled me from my seat.

Portsmouth, Virginia, 1954
Uncombed Hair

I stood before my classmates,
shoulders erect,
body rigid.
Miss Wood plowed through my hair
with her pink plastic comb
pulling tangles like weeds
from Mrs. Harris's flower bed.
Sandy lifted her hand to hide a smirk
behind her clean fingernails.
Margie dropped her head
on the table and sniffled.
Buddy glared at Miss Wood
and removed his clenched fists
from the tabletop to his lap.
I wanted to scream out
from the pain
and the embarrassment,
but my relentless pride refused
to indulge her, until silent tears
betrayed me.

Portsmouth, Virginia, 1954
Naptime

With our heads down on our sweaty arms after recess,
the cool wooden tables soothed our bodies.
The classroom fan inspected us like a nosy
neighbor as it swung to and fro,
vibrated on its perch atop the metal file cabinet,
stirring only the hot air on the ceiling.
Sunshine streamed in through the tall
classroom windows, cooking
the window-sill geraniums.
Two captive flies explored the glass panes.
Miss Wood's gray ringlets bounced wildly
as she struggled with the uncooperative
dark-green window shades.
Buddy wiped his blue flannel
sleeve upward to stop his runny nose
and to compensate
for a much-needed haircut
all in one swift motion.
"I h-h-hate her," he whispered.

Portsmouth, Virginia, 1954
Paulette Lucille

At school
I envied the Lindas and Sandras
with their popular names
and their matching sweater sets.
I watched them as they raced home
after school to their two-story houses
surrounded by tall pine trees
that swayed with the wind
and red roses that climbed
the trellises, reaching into the sky
like Jack's beanstalk.
I heard their jump-rope chants
on the sidewalk.

On Saturdays,
I saw them with their daddies
in the Sixth Avenue Pharmacy,
where they whined for scoops
of chocolate ice cream
on brown sugar cones.

But like the number three
in my favorite fairy tales,
my name was sprinkled
with fairy dust
and hope.

My name clicked like the castanets
of the flamenco dancers
on the *Ed Sullivan Show*
as they twirled across Mrs. Harris's
black and white television screen.

My name embodied the hint of possibility,
and the awareness of what might be.
My mother loved lost souls,
lost causes, and late bloomers.
My name reflected my mother's
belief in dreams.

Carefully, I printed my name
in perfect manuscript letters
across the top of my paper
in my first-grade class.

Paulette Lucille
    patience,
        perseverance,
            persistence.

Portsmouth, Virginia, 1954
Paper Dolls

Lying on her stomach and peering
into the dark space
beneath her bed,
Judy reached for the
Blumberg's Department Store box,
dragged it out to the center
of the cool hardwood floor
and lifted the top,
revealing an array of colorful
characters, carefully cut
from paper prisons.
She dressed them one by one,
propping them against the
backdrop of her pink chenille bedspread.

Smiling movie stars in mink coats
and feathered capes displayed diamond
bracelets on long-gloved arms.
A shy bride in white lace posed
with a bouquet of roses and ribbons
alongside her pastel bridesmaids
crowned with satin roses and tulle net hats.
A handsome man in sleek striped pants
and a long-tailed tuxedo posed with
one hand in his pocket.
A dimpled girl in a plaid skirt
and knee socks carried a bundle of books
in a leather strap.

"Come on," Judy urged,
"You can help."
I reached into the box and removed
a well-worn doll, a brunette in a white slip
and high-heeled shoes,
her head bent backwards from frequent use.
I carefully folded the tabs on her blue gingham
house dress and white ruffled apron.
"That's the mother doll," Judy said.
I propped her against the bedspread with the others
and searched through the box for the father,
who I was sure would be wearing a robe
and warm brown slippers, and
holding a pipe.

Portsmouth, Virginia, 1954

Old People

Mrs. Frost lived across the street from us.
She was a frail old lady
who I guessed was
about 102 years old.
I watched her hobbling down
the sidewalk with her cane
in her tattered, old green coat
and pointy-toed shoes.
She always carried an empty corn can
for spitting her snuff.
When her short gray hair
grew too long to suit her,
she cut it off herself and
didn't care it if it was even or not.
She just put on her red
polka-dotted kerchief and
tied it under her chin—
giving her the appearance of an
ancient Christmas tree coming
down the street.

Mr. Frost, her son, still lived with his mother,
and came along when she came to visit.
He was a large man with straggly gray hair that
looked like his mother cut it.
He wore plaid flannel shirts
and denim overalls with straps
where he rested his thumbs.

Sometimes he hooked his thumbs
on the straps of the bib
and moved his fingers for emphasis
as he talked.

I didn't mind Mrs. Frost,
but I didn't like her son.
He grabbed at me saying,
"Come here, Missy."
He tried to get me to sit on his lap
coming at me with his big
cat-like paws, trying to tickle me—
but I squirmed away from him,
and his rough unshaven face,
his sour body odor, his coffee breath.

Mrs. Frost told Mama about the
letter she received from Oral Roberts.
"He wants me to go to the Holy Land
with him," she said, "but I can't go
on a trip like that!"

Mama tried to explain that Oral Roberts
was a missionary,
and he was going on a mission trip.

Trying to be helpful,
I said that he probably wanted her
to donate money for his ministry,
but Mrs. Frost became angry
and started spitting her snuff

in the empty corn can that she
carried with her everywhere.
She jumped to her feet, glaring at me,
"Come on, Sonny. We'll come back
another time when this one is not
here," she said, pointing at me.

When she left, Mama said,
"See? I told you.
When grownups are talking,
you need to keep your mouth shut.
When will you ever learn? You are
too outspoken."

*And when will old men learn to keep
their hands to themselves?*

Portsmouth, Virginia, 1954

Growing Pains

In deepest sleep
they pulled at my muscles
tearing the cries from my throat.
Mama came to my bedside where
she sat and rubbed oil of wintergreen
on the tight knots in my legs
until my tears subsided.

I asked Mama,
"Why does growing
have to hurt so much?"

"Shhh," Mama said,
"Go back to sleep."

Portsmouth, Virginia, 1954
Judy's Homework

Peering over Judy's shoulder,
I watched as she carefully drew
the dark blue ink
into her new pen.
Then Judy placed the ink bottle
on the table next to her mother's
pink velvet chair and
returned to her homework
at the dining room table.

I could not wait to be
a big girl like Judy and
have my own pen and my own
homework.
I could not wait to carry big books
with big words, words I could read.
Maybe I could have
a composition notebook
to write my stories and poems.

I could see myself sitting alongside Judy
at the dining room table,
wearing a green-and-blue
plaid skirt with pleats
and a soft blue sweater
with pearl buttons,

lots of clean white paper
stacked in front of me,
and me with my own pen
writing my own
homework.

I reached out to touch the bottle.
cool on my fingertips,
lovely visions in my head,
when Mrs. Harris entered the room
startling me
and the ink bottle
tumbled off the table,
splashing ink
on her pink velvet chair.

Portsmouth, Virginia, 1954
I Am a Big Girl Now

Mama said I could not stay with Mrs. Harris
anymore while she's at work—
not since I spilled the ink and
ruined Mrs. Harris's pink velvet chair.

Mama cried and said that I am a big girl now,
I am seven.
She said I could stay by myself now,
because she could not pay $65 to replace the chair
and pay a babysitter to take care of me.
Mrs. Powell, our upstairs neighbor,
would check on me.

I would miss playing with Judy and her
paper dolls, and I would miss Mrs. Harris's
whipped creamed potatoes.
I would miss watching the *Mickey Mouse Club*
in the afternoons.
We didn't have a television.
But Mama said I am a big girl now
I would keep myself busy.

Portsmouth, Virginia, 1954
Keeping Busy

I turned on my happy face
like the neon ice cream sign
at the Sixth Avenue Pharmacy.
I kissed Mama goodbye
as she promised a visit
from Mrs. Powell,
our neighbor lady
but I switched off my neon smile
when the door closed.

I imitated all the instruments
and sang along with Mama's
78 rpm records while
dancing with my shadow.

Flipping the pages
of the Sears Roebuck Wish Book,
I wished for a television
with rabbit ears,
a modern kitchen range to
replace our hot plate,
and real cloth curtains
where the plastic ones hung.

When I tired of this game
I climbed into bed,
where I examined
the wallpaper patterns,

bouquets of daisies, and
picked at the seams
where the glue
had released its hold.
I stripped away the loose paper
in dime-sized chunks,
exposing the layers beneath.
I changed to baby-blue
flannel pajamas
with cherry cough syrup stains
and investigated my legs,
jump-rope scars
and sidewalk scabs,
badges of neighborhood play.

Carefully, I pulled at the edges,
exposing the prickly pink skin
beneath the brown scabs,
pulling until droplets of blood
appeared.

When Mama returned,
she tucked the covers
up around my chin,
oblivious to the bloody stains
on my legs or the loneliness
that filled my life.

Portsmouth, Virginia, 1954

Orphanage

"Orphanage!"
Richard Fitzgerald taunted me
and pulled my braids
when the teacher turned
to the blackboard.

"Orphanage!"
He called
from behind the bushes at recess
interrupting the girls' game
of blacktop hopscotch.

"Orphanage!"
He jeered
from across Sixth Avenue
on the walk home from school.

"What does orphanage mean?"
I asked Mama.
Mama said,
"It is a place
for children without parents."

"Orphanage!"
He hissed from between clenched teeth
as he passed my table
in the cafeteria.

I swallowed chocolate milk
through a paper straw
and answered through lips
stained with grape jam
and peanut butter.

"I am not a place.
I am a person."

Georgia, 1929

Georgia Orphanage

Mama told me about her time in
the orphanage, when she
was less than two years old.
She didn't remember much,
but she knew
they housed children
whose parents who were
missing
disabled
imprisoned
mentally ill
      dead.

Children came without
clothing, food,
education…
without hope.

In thirty years
fourteen-hundred
boys and girls found
warmth, faith
determination, and
courage there.
They found a home.

The older children
watched after
the younger ones
The younger children played
outside on the swings, slides,
and a little Ferris wheel.

All the children
shared chores: laundry,
sewing, canning,
gardening, picking cotton,
cleaning the house.

They ate their meals
    together in the dining room,
prayed
    together in the chapel,
learned
    together in the school room,
slept
    together in the dormitory.

They were a
family.

Georgia, 1929

Aunt Jenny and the Biscuits

I asked Aunt Jenny if she remembered
living in the orphanage. She told me that
when she was six years old,
she squirreled away food
for her baby sisters—
Audrey and my mama,
Onelia.

One night she slipped
into the kitchen,
creeping across the
creaky floors
while the sounds of sleep
filled the house.
She returned with biscuits:
crumbly, stale, leftover.
Mama and Aunt Audrey
ate them.

The next morning, Miz Lillian,
the cook,
told the children
around the table
about the biscuit thief.
Jenny listened with
wide eyes.

Miz Lillian asked Jenny
to stay after breakfast
to help her clear the table.
She asked if Jenny had
stolen the biscuits.
Jenny looked at her,
her face flaming red,
and shook her head.
Miz Lillian smiled and said,
"I am so glad you didn't take
the biscuits, Jenny. Because
when I made them, I went
into the nursery."

Jenny tilted her head.
Miz Lillian smiled as she leaned over
and looked directly into Jenny's eyes.

"Do you know why I went
to the nursery, Jenny?"
Jenny shook her head.

"I got a dirty diaper
and put the SHIT in my biscuits!"
Then Miz Lillian screamed
directly into Jenny's face,
"Don't ever steal from
my kitchen again!"

Jenny ran straight
to the bathroom gagging.
While she vomited,
the cook's rollicking laughter
filled the kitchen.

Jenny never stole
biscuits again.
        Not ever.

Portsmouth, Virginia, 1954
I Wondered

Mama lived in the orphanage,
but she was too young
to remember
those days.

I wondered
        if Mama was separated
        from her sisters and placed
        in the nursery with the infants.

I wondered
        if Papa ever visited his girls
        over the next two years.

I wondered
        if Mama even knew
        her daddy when he came back
        to get them.

I wondered.

And I was grateful
that I never had
to live in an orphanage
like my Mama
and her sisters.

Portsmouth, Virginia, 1955
Playing with Fire

I sipped from my Pepsi bottle
and bit into my MoonPie
as I read the captions under the pictures
in Mama's *True Confessions* magazine.
I skimmed the stories for the bad parts
and read them with wide eyes.
I didn't need a babysitter.
Babysitters were for babies,
and I was not a baby

The forbidden match pad beckoned
from the coffee table.
A woman in a bathing suit sat in an
oversized shoe, her long legs and high heels
swinging in the air above her:
"The Silver Slipper Lounge," she advertised...
"where friends meet friends."

Red sparks danced across the pad
as I struck the match
just beneath the woman in the shoe.
I held the matchstick and stared into the flame
for as long as I could, until the flame reached
my fingertips. Then I blew it out before
I dropped the blackened stick into the wastebasket.

Once again, I struck beneath the woman in the shoe
and watched the flame, blue-orange-yellow-red
until a knock on the door startled me,
and I dropped the burning matchstick into
the wastebasket before I rushed to answer the door.
Flames grew in the waste basket.
Mrs. Powell rushed in,
removed the waste basket with the flames,
and glared at my surprised face.

Portsmouth, Virginia, 1955
Guilt

I swore to Mama that
I didn't play with matches.
She showed me the evidence
in the waste basket,
and then she cried
some more.

What if you had burned
the house down?

Why couldn't you be a good girl
so that I can work?

I thought you were a big girl
and could take care
of yourself.

I thought
I could trust you.

What if Mrs. Powell had not
come to check on you?

Aren't you ashamed of yourself?

Yes.
Very.
Ashamed.

Portsmouth, Virginia, 1955

School Pictures

I didn't favor Mama at all.
I hated my tanned skin and
my cheekbones,
the moles scattered
over my body.
Mama said they were
beauty marks.
But I didn't feel beautiful.
I yearned for my mother's creamy
complexion and movie-star looks.

Mama said I looked like John Henry.
I didn't remember him,
but I saw a picture of him once.
He was standing by the roller coaster
wearing a rumpled shirt
with his sleeves pushed up, his hair
hanging in his eyes,
his face all scrunched up
like he wasn't particularly happy
about having his picture made.
I wondered if Mama was with him that day,
but I didn't dare ask.

The girl in my school pictures
showed her gums when she smiled.
I hated her looks.
I said, "It doesn't even look like me."

Mama said,
"Do you think the camera tells a lie?"
I practiced my smile in the mirror
But no matter how I tried,
I couldn't erase the hurt in my eyes.

Father Knows Best

Perched on the windowsill
of the upstairs bathroom
that we shared with Mrs. Powell,
I had a perfect view
of the whole block from
between the branches
of the sycamore tree.

Margie's father was coming home
from work, pulling his new Ford
into the driveway across the street.
Margie glided down the sidewalk
on her new blue bike,
swaying side to side as she stood
to push the pedals with all her weight.
Margie's mother greeted them at the door,
Margie clinging to her daddy's legs
when he leaned over to kiss her mom.
The door closed.

Mrs. Powell rapped on the bathroom door:
"Are you going to stay in there all day?"
The spell was broken.
I waited for her to knock once more
before opening the door
and stomping out
with my hands on my hips.
Can't a person have any privacy in this place?

Portsmouth, Virginia, 1955

Romantic Fever

Dr. Goldman came to our apartment
when Mama called and told him
about my fever, 102 degrees.
He questioned Mama about the sore
throat I had a few weeks before,
touched my sore ankles, my knees,
my elbows, and my wrists,
observed the red splotches on my skin,
and diagnosed my rheumatic fever—
a condition that would keep me in
bed and at home
for months.

He gave me a penicillin shot in my butt,
and told Mama he would be back in
three weeks to give me another.
Dr. Goldman emphasized to Mama
that my heart could be permanently
damaged if she didn't follow his directions.
No problem.
I could hardly move anyway.

I slept while Mama was
working, but I had the radio
right beside
my bed for company.

I listened to soap operas,
The Guiding Light
and *Young Doctor Malone.*

My Granny came from Georgia to see me,
along with a bunch of aunts and uncles.
She brought me a tiny glass figurine
of a white dog with brown spots
chewing on a shoe. A pink blossom adorned
his head. He sat at my bedside
and watched me as he held on to his shoe.
He never barked.
He didn't need any special treatment.
Mama said he was the perfect pet
and a good listener.

When Mama left for work, she
propped me up with pillows,
made sure I had sharpened
pencils and a pad of paper to copy
the cursive alphabet in the back
of my second-grade spelling book—
and I stayed in bed like I was told,
cause romantic fever was nothing
to play around with.

One day I pushed my pencil
into the fabric that covered the speakers
on the radio, disturbing the tubes inside,
and it stopped working.
When Mama discovered what I had done,

She asked, "Why did you do that?"
I said, "I don't know."

And I didn't know.

I didn't know why I was alone for hours every day
with only a radio to keep me company.
I didn't know why she had to leave me.
I didn't know why I couldn't go to school.
I didn't know why I was sick.
I didn't know why all my friends
had two parents
and

I didn't have
a father.

Shelby Jean

My cousin, Shelby Jean,
came all the way
from South Carolina
to take care of me
during summer vacation
while Mama worked.

Shelby Jean, who was fourteen,
sat on the front porch swing reading
True Romance magazines
while I played
with my neighborhood friends,
Nancy and Buddy.
We played hopscotch
on the sidewalk and Monopoly
on the cool floor of the front porch.
Sometimes we caught June bugs
and tied string around their legs
so we could swing them and
watch them fly.

"Hey, Paula," Shelby Jean said in her
South Carolina drawl
as she leaned over the porch railing,
"Why don't you go to the store,
and get me a MoonPie and a Co-Cola?
Get something for yourself, too.
Jus' tell 'em to put it on your mama's bill."

Off I ran across the street to Bristow's Store
with Nancy and Buddy following.
We bought penny candy for me and Nancy,
bubble gum and baseball cards for Buddy,
and, of course, Shelby Jean's MoonPie
and Co-Cola.

Day after day for several
weeks we went to Bristow's.
until one day I bought Dreamsicles
for me and Nancy,
comic books for Buddy,
and Lucky Strikes for Shelby Jean,
since she was learning to smoke.

"Jus' put it on the bill, Mr. Bristow."
His bushy eyebrows
wrinkled up on his brow
like Groucho Marx.
"OK," he said, "but tell your mama
to come and see me
when she gets home from work."

 I did.

Mama came
dragging up the steps
from Bristow's
with the bill in her hand
and tears in her eyes.
"Shelby Jean," she said.

"You are going to
have to go home, honey.
I can't afford to have you babysit."

Portsmouth, Virginia, 1955

Snowy Day

Outside on Queen Street
children with arms and legs
bundled like sausages
slipped along icy walkways
in shiny red galoshes.

I watched from the window as
Nancy and Buddy waved with wet
pink hands and smiled with
chapped faces.
Nancy paused to wipe her runny
nose on the sleeve of her coat
when Sonny McGee pitched
a snowball that caught her
off guard and left a red mark
on her face.
Sonny ran while Nancy and Buddy
followed him with snowballs
in their fists.

The cold windowpane
soothed my feverish cheeks,
but Mama arrived and chased
me back to bed,
wrapping my chest with
a soft cloth soaked in Vicks.
I breathed in deeply and inhaled
the menthol, while Mama poured

water in the pan on the oil stove.
I heard the sizzle and watched
the steam rise, as I drifted
into sleep.

Portsmouth, Virginia, 1955

Homemade Valentines

I was cutting out my Valentines when
a loud knock on the door interrupted
my concentration. I jerked open the door,
spied their backs as they ran away.
I found two hearts cut from notebook paper
and colored with yellow and green crayon
on the floor in the hallway.

On the front porch, I heard them
scurrying away. I stepped out of the door
and peeped into the dark streets.
"Hey! I see you!" I shouted.
I heard snickers from behind Mr. Harris's car.

I thought the Valentines were from
Nancy and Buddy, but I checked each number
on my code breaker.
2-21-4-4-25
Yep, that's Buddy.
14-1-14-3-25
N-A-N-C-Y
I hurried to finish signing
my Valentines,
16-1-21-12-5-20-20-5

I looked out the window
to see the kids moving
up and down Queen Street,

dropping their Valentines
on the doorsteps,
stomping on the porches
or banging on the doors
before running to hide.
I hurried out of the apartment
to join the fun.

Portsmouth, Virginia, 1955
Mama, May I?

Mama,
may I
have
a hula
hoop?
All
the
kids
have
them.
And I—
I want
one,
too.
A red one!

Mama.
may I
have
a dog?
I want—
I want
a little
dog
to sleep
with
at night.

Nancy
has
a little
dog.
And I—
I want one,
too.
A spotted one.

Mama,
may I
have
a bicycle?
Margie
has a blue
bike.
I want—
I want one,
too.
I can
ride
everywhere
on my bike.
Blue.

Mama,
may I
have a
hula
hoop?

They go
round
and
round.
Spinning
faster
and faster.

May
I please
have
a hula
hoop
like
all the
other
kids?

Portsmouth, Virginia, 1955
Scotty

Scotty worked with Mama.
She talked funny
because she came from another country.

Her daughter, Ella, was my age
and she could talk funny
like her mother
when she wanted to.

One day in late summer
Mama came home
with Scotty and Ella
and a couple of bags
with all their clothing.

Mama said they were going
to stay with us for a while.
Ella could be like my sister.
       Nobody asked me if I wanted a sister.

Mama and Scotty would share
the rent and the bills.
Ella and I would share clothes.
Ella could be like my sister.
       Nobody asked me if I wanted a sister.

Mama had my new school clothes
and winter coat on layaway.

She went back to Woolworth's
and changed the layaway.
Now I had half as many clothes.
Ella and I had matching outfits
and coats
like sisters
     But nobody asked me if I wanted a sister.

I didn't want to dress like Ella.
I didn't want to walk to school with her
I didn't want to play with her.
I didn't want to live with her.

I told Mama I didn't like Ella
And didn't want her for a sister.

Mama said they didn't have
anywhere to go:
    no house,
       no money,
         no food,

                no family.

Ella's dad was mean.
He was always
   threatening,
     screaming
       yelling
         hitting.

Mama asked
"How would you feel?
Would you want someone
　　　　to help,
　　　　to share,
　　　　to listen,
　　　　to care?"

I thought about it and
said, "Well, I guess so.
But no one asked me if I wanted a sister."

Then Mama explained,
"Sometimes in life we get things we didn't ask for."

Dinner with Clark Gable

"Ring, ring," said Mama.
"Oh, I hear the telephone," said Scotty
in her funny-sounding Scottish voice.

Ella and I rolled our eyes
and raised our eyebrows,
knowing they were playing
their silly game with us again.

"Hello," said Mama with her
hand against her ear like a real telephone.
"Oh, hello, Clark!
I'm sorry, I can't have dinner
with you tonight. I'm eating
with my girls."

Pause.

"Oh, we are having steak and mashed
potatoes and the most delicious
dessert you have ever seen."

Ella and I looked down at our tomato soup
and started to giggle.

Pause.

"Yes, Clark, I would love to ride in
your fancy car some other time."

"Ask him if he can get me a date,"
said Scotty.

As we continued to laugh
at our silly mothers,
Ella and I started to eat our soup.

They continued with their antics
until we had finished eating
and left the room to do our homework

like sisters.

Portsmouth, Virginia, 1955
New Beginnings

September marched into our lives
like new shoes on hardwood floors,
and I wondered how summer
could have slipped away so easily.
With brightly colored cotton dresses
just out of layaway
from the five-and-ten-cent store
and satin ribbons dangling
from my pin-curled hair,
I joined my classmates at Sixth Avenue
Elementary School as we
lifted our faces to our nation's flag
and our hearts raced like runaway horses
as we sang.
We believed in new beginnings.
School was a place you came
to learn who you were,
and what you could become.

Mr. Murphy, Danny, Colorado…
Miss Wood…
     All

             distant memories now.

Ella's Daddy

He came to visit his daughter.
>   *She didn't want to see her dad.*

He came to bring his wife back home.
>   *She didn't want to go home with him.*

He told Mama he loved his family.
>   *They told Mama he was lying.*

He said he would never hit his wife or child.
>   *They showed Mama their bruises.*

Mama said it would not be
right to keep a man from his child
        as they packed up to leave.

I listened carefully to what they said
and counted the times
I remembered seeing my father

        on one hand.

Portsmouth, Virginia, 1955
Christmas Eve

I pretended to be asleep
so that Santa could come
and bring my toys.
But I heard Mama and the soft
sounds of wrapping paper
in the living room,
heard her struggling
to put together the pieces
of the metal dollhouse.
I heard her whispering to herself
as she read the directions
and tried to match the places
where the roof connected
with the walls,
heard the metal as it rattled
where the top floor connected
to the bottom floor,
heard her tears
when her frustration
rubbed up against her wish
for a perfect Christmas
for her girl.

Portsmouth, Virginia, 1955
Contradictions

My teacher, Mrs. Short
was very tall.

She said the only important thing
was that we do our best,
but when I made mistakes,
she marked my paper
with a red pencil.

She told us reading
was most important,
But Dick and Jane were
not allowed to leave the classroom,
and I did not have any books at home.

Mrs. Short said
that girls could do anything they want,
but she packed up her desk drawer
in a pasteboard box
and left us behind.
She was going to have a baby,
and women were not allowed to teach
when they were in a family way.

Portsmouth, Virginia, 1955
Recess Time

When the boys' basketball bounced
into our jump-rope line,
I snatched it up and ran.
Richard Fitzgerald chased me
and knocked me down on the pavement,
scraping my knees and hurting my pride.
His cold blue eyes blazing
from his sweaty red face,
he screamed,
"Girls don't play basketball!"

"Well, maybe girls would
like to play sometimes, too!"
I answered his back in defeat
as he walked away
with the ball under his arm,
me, still sitting on the blacktop.

"Little Sally Ann,
sittin' in the sand,
weepin' and a-cryin'
for a nice young man."

"Cinderella
dressed in yellow,
went upstairs
to kiss her fella."

Jump-rope jingles
and playground games
shaped our lives.

We already knew as girls
what the world
expected of us as women.

Portsmouth, Virginia, 1955

Miracle Vaccine

The line reached
across the classroom
and down the hallway.
Children
with sleeves rolled up.
Images of iron lungs
and leg braces
trumped the threat
of the needle.
I told Sandy
about the doctor
who said I could not take
the polio vaccine.

"Why?" she asked.

"Because," I said
"My heart is weak
from romantic fever."

Decisions, Decisions

Mama swore that she would
never marry again,
but she had several boyfriends
who came home from work
with her and visited in the kitchen
when I was supposed to be asleep.

Once I got up and peeped through
the kitchen door.
A man was sitting at the kitchen table.
Mama was sitting on his lap
and kissing him,
her fingers in his hair.
I rushed back to bed and pulled
up the covers around my chin.
Eyes closed tightly.

Soon they came into the room
where Mama and I slept in twin beds.
"This here's my girl," Mama said.
"Well, she's a mighty pretty little thing," he said,
before leaving the apartment
through the front door.

Later, Mama told me that she had
two boyfriends.
They had both been married before.
One was younger than she

and drove a really nice car.
She laughed and said,
"He is pretty wild."
Then she added,
"He is a lot of fun
and makes me laugh."
The other boyfriend was older than
she was. She had met him
through Aunt Marie.
"He's very smart," she said,
"and he seems more dependable."

They both wanted to marry her.
"Which one should I marry?"
she asked.

Don't ask me.
You are the one
who will have
to live with him.

Norfolk, Virginia, 1956
The Hillbilly Cat

Crowds of country music fans
filled the seats below us.
We squinted to see the stage
from high in the balcony.

Cheers and applause for
each performance—
Kitty Wells, the Carter Family,
and many others—
until they finally announced
the Hillbilly Cat
singing his new song,
"Heartbreak Hotel."

I whisper-sang along
with every note.
He sang and wiggled,
and he sang some more.
He broke his guitar strings,
and they brought him
another guitar.

Mama and I slipped out the back,
and waited by the stage door
until he appeared to sign autographs.
I handed him the bright yellow program
with his photograph
on the back.

He scribbled his name,
Elvis Presley,
across the image of his face.

I could not believe
he was so famous
yet my cursive
was far superior.

Portsmouth, Virginia, 1956
The Marriage

Mama married Doc,
the more dependable one,
and he moved in with us
on Queen Street
until they could get a larger
apartment.

Mama said his mother had
named him after the doctor
who delivered him.
I had never heard of anyone
named Doc before except the
guy in the Seven Dwarfs.

Mama said that we would
not have to worry about
the bills anymore.
He would take care of us.

Mama laid down the law to him
before they married:
"You will never adopt Paulette,
she will always be allowed to
visit her people in Georgia,
and you will never lay a hand on her,
or I will kill you."

And he never did.

Portsmouth, Virginia, 1956
Doc and the Tomboy

Doc bought us a television;
he helped me with my homework;
sometimes he cooked for us,
and cleaned the house for Mama.
I never heard of a man
who cooked and cleaned,
but Doc did.
Mama was very happy.

Pretty soon Mama was going to have
a baby, and she stopped working.
We moved into an apartment
right across Queen Street
over top of Bristow's Grocery Store
where I had a large bedroom
all to myself and a spotted spaniel named
Fluffy to sleep on the end
of my bed.

Mama brought Katie home
from the hospital.
She was a tiny baby
who looked like Susie,
the doll that I had lost
years before.

Katie cried and pooped
and Mama fed her, kissed her, hugged her,
changed her diapers, and held her.
Doc rocked her in the rocking chair
he bought for Mama.
Mama dressed her up in lacy pink gowns
with matching caps, wrapped her in
soft flannel blankets,
and they took lots of pictures of her.

When they were watching
The Miss America Pageant,
Doc said, "That's our girl, someday.
Katie will not be a tomboy
like Paulette."

Portsmouth, Virginia, 1956

Moving Away

Doc was in the Navy, and they told him
they needed him to move to a new place—
Charleston, South Carolina.
Mama didn't want to leave her family again,
but she said,
"It will be an adventure."

I remembered the other adventure,
the Greyhound bus ride from Colorado,
the desperate phone call to Papa
from the phone booth…Mr. Murphy…
Danny.

But this move was different.
The Navy men came and moved our boxes.
We got in the car with baby Katie,
my dog, Fluffy, and my goldfish.
Mama said we could just give the dog
and the fish away. But Doc said
"No," as he patted me on the back.
"These things are important
to Paulette."

Charleston, South Carolina, 1957

Settling In

Mama said that we would live
in Navy housing
on the outskirts of Charleston.
There would be lots of children
for me to play with.
But when we arrived,
there were no Navy apartments
available.

Doc found us a place to live
in a historic house on Atlantic Street
in downtown Charleston,
right off the Battery.

When our furniture arrived,
they moved us in.
Mama gave me the bedroom
with two big French windows
opening onto the back porch
with a view of her wringer
washing machine.
I opened the windows wide,
inviting breezes
to relieve the Charleston humidity.

Mama always wanted a vegetable garden,
but the high brick walls covered in ivy
outside my window,

provided a privacy garden,
not the garden of Mama's dreams.

I made up my twin beds
with the sheets and bedspreads
that Mama gave me,
put away my clothes
in the drawers and closets,
and stuffed my hula hoop
under my bed right beside
the shoebox
with my movie star pictures
and my autographed photo
of Elvis Presley.
Then I watched
the baby for Mama
while she unpacked.
             Where are
                          the children?

Mama's Cookin'

Country cooking was Mama's style:
fried chicken and fried okra,
butter beans and turnip greens,
mashed potatoes and sliced tomatoes,
and cakes made
from Betty Crocker cake mixes.

Mama didn't cook with recipes.
She added in a little of this
and a little of that and
her meals were always scrumptious.

Doc smiled and rubbed his tummy
as I washed the dishes after dinner.
Mama rested in front of the TV
and Doc took care of the baby.

Mama said she wanted a whole house
full of children in the country someday.
Doc just laughed.

Then I put Katie in the stroller
and took her for a walk
in the streets of Charleston.

Charleston, South Carolina, 1957
The Battery

Out our front door,
walking about a half block
up our cobblestone street,
I strolled baby Katie
to the Battery, where the salt
air breezes cooled our faces.
The fragrant water sloshed
against the sides of the seawall.
Bunches of green bananas floated by.
What faraway waters brought
them here?

Farther out, Fort Sumter peered
back at me, the site where
the first shots were fired
in the War Between the States.
That's what Doc said.

He also told me to call him Daddy.
It felt a little bit strange—
I had never called anyone
Daddy. But Mama said I should,
because surely the baby would start
calling him Doc if she heard me.

Charleston, South Carolina, 1957
Exploring Charleston

Up and down the streets of Charleston
on my bicycle, I found the children
at the Recreation Center
just around the corner from our house,
where I learned to play ping-pong
and dominoes—and later came in first place
in the Chinese Checkers Tournament.

I wandered through museums and
gardens, enjoying the freedom
of hours on my own. Collected
brochures from the travel agencies
and hotel lobbies, where I stopped
to drink from water fountains.

One of my favorite places was
a record shop on King Street, with
little booths where I could listen
to my favorite songs, carefully
lifting the needle to avoid scratches.
Whenever I managed
to save ninety-eight cents, I bought a record.
My Elvis collection was growing!

Gift stores and antique shops,
a never-ending array of places to explore.
Charleston grew on me like Spanish moss
on an ancient oak tree.

Charleston, South Carolina, 1957
Mama's Driving

Mama didn't think she could drive
a car, but Daddy taught her to
drive his 1950 gray Oldsmobile.
Then she took Katie and me for
Sunday rides, driving to Folly Beach,
with our arms hung out the windows—
catching the wind and
watching the palmetto trees
sway in the salty breezes.

Sometimes we picked up hitchhikers
and learned their stories on the way.
Finally, Mama got up her nerve
and drove us across the Cooper River Bridge,
praying all the way that we would make it across
that high and narrow bridge with that huge
curve right in the middle.

When we reached the north shore,
Mama called Daddy on a pay phone
from Mount Pleasant, telling him to get a cab
and come drive us home because she was
too afraid to drive back across that crazy bridge.

Charleston, South Carolina, 1957

Mama's Naps

When Daddy went to work,
Mama took frequent naps
in between her TV programs.
Soon she said she was going to have
another baby, and I would have to help more
because she was exhausted all the time.

I fed Katie, changed her diapers, combed
her hair, and dressed her in cute
little baby outfits that Mama found on sale
like her linen navy-blue sailor dress,
black patent leather Mary Janes and white,
lacy socks, topped off with her straw hat.
I felt like I had another baby doll
when I strolled her down the street
to the park while Mama napped.

Goodbye, Fluffy

One day when I arrived home from school
I found a strange woman in our house.
She said her name was Peggy,
and she met Mama in the park.
She was holding Katie.
Mama was in the kitchen crying.
Mama had taken my dog, Fluffy,
to the vet and had her put to sleep.

"Why, Mama?" I cried.
Mama said Fluffy had eaten some
rat poison that our landlord
used to keep pests away.
Fluffy was very sick
and would never get better.
It was the only thing to do.
I ran to my bedroom and flung
myself on my bed crying.

Peggy came into my room
still holding Katie.
"Straighten up!" she demanded.
"Your mom feels bad enough.
You don't need to make it any harder on her."

Harder on her? Harder on her?
I thought.
Well, who are you, anyway?

But I got up off my bed and said,
"Yes, ma'am."

Then I walked by the kitchen door,
saw Mama still crying at the table,
went out the back door
and rode my bike down the street
wiping my tears on my shirt sleeves.

Charleston, South Carolina, 1957
Sixth Grade

Mrs. Mormon knew everything.
She told us about the dirty Communists and
the Cold War, and about Sputnik
spinning through its orbit in the heavens.
She showed us how to duck and cover,
using our desks for protection
in case of nuclear attack.

Mrs. Mormon told us about floating
across the dance floor at the Inaugural Ball
when her friend, Fritz Hollings, became governor
of South Carolina.

Mrs. Mormon told us about Edward R. Murrow
and his television show.
She said no good could come
from a man named Fidel who had the poor taste
to appear on television in his pajamas.

Mrs. Mormon didn't like the spelling sentences
I wrote using Elvis Presley
as the subject of every single sentence,
but she let me write a play for the class
and choose my classmates as performers.
And she let me stay after school and help
erase the blackboards and clean the erasers.
Then she waved to me from the second floor
as I rode away on my bike.

Charleston, South Carolina, 1957

Mrs. Rhodes

Mrs. Rhodes, my Sunday School
teacher, had long blond curly hair
and wore the prettiest dresses with
matching high heels. She pulled off
her lacy little gloves when she played
the piano for us to sing.
"Leaning on the Everlasting Arms."

The flowers on her hat bounced
with the rhythm of the keyboard.
We all loved Mrs. Rhodes, and we loved
the way she played the piano for us.

Mrs. Rhodes said the most beautiful
prayers. All the girls wanted to be
just like Mrs. Rhodes, and have a
husband like Mr. Rhodes, tall and
handsome. We watched them from
the balcony as they sat together
holding hands during the services.
If the doors to the church
were open, they were there—
and I knew it, because I was there as well.

Sunday School and preaching afterwards
on Sunday morning. Training Union
and preaching on Sunday nights,
prayer meeting on Wednesday nights

sometimes with Bible drills— and
I was very good at finding
Bible verses in a flash!

Girl's Auxiliary Missionary Meeting
on Tuesday afternoons, and Junior Choir
practice on Thursday afternoons.

First Baptist Church.
A hop, skip, and a jump away.
My home away from home.

Charleston, South Carolina, 1958

Piano Love

"Mama, can I go to school at my church?"

"No," Mama said.

"But they have a real nice school, Mama,
and a lot of the girls in my Sunday School class
go to school there."

"No," Mama said. "It costs lots of money."

"Well, can I take piano lessons? Mrs. Rhodes teaches
piano lessons after school there."

"No," Mama said. "It costs lots of money."

"Well, I could save my allowance."

"No," Mama said. "It would not be enough.
And besides, you would be just like all the other kids.
You would not want to practice."

"But I promise, Mama. I will practice."

"How are you going to practice?" Mama said.
"We don't have a piano. Now quit bothering
me or you won't be going to church there
anymore."

Charleston, South Carolina, 1957
Tamra's Birthday

All the girls were talking
about Tamra's birthday.
She was having a party
and everyone was invited.
Everyone except me.

Tamra was a tiny girl
with blond hair and a
smooth tanned complexion.
She wore all the latest
fashions.

A boy-girl party with snacks
to eat and records
for dancing
and everyone was invited.
Everyone except me.

I had a book, almost new:
Ginny Gordon and the Lending Library.
I wrapped it up
and took it to school.
I gave it to Tamra with a note
telling her that I hoped she
had a happy birthday.

"Oh," she said. "Thank you so much.
Would you like to come to my birthday
party on Saturday night?"

"Sure." I said in my best surprised tone.
"But I'll have to ask my mama."

When I asked Mama,
she said "No. Doc and I are going
out to a dance Saturday night,
and you are going to babysit."

It's OK. I didn't want to read
that Ginny Gordon book anyway.

Charleston, South Carolina, 1957
The Fall

One day while Mama napped,
I took Katie down Atlantic Street
in her stroller. She smiled and laughed
at people who stopped to say
how cute she was with her big blue eyes,
dimpled chin, and two little teeth
pushing up from her bottom gums.

She loved the ride and giggled
when I pushed her quickly on the walkway.
I started to run and push the stroller.
Shoving as hard as I could, I let go
of the stroller and watched it
speed along without me, as I ran to catch up.
Katie laughed even harder.

Once again, I ran and shoved the stroller.
This time the wheels caught between
two stones on the walkway and the stroller
tipped forward. Katie tumbled out onto the
walkway and screamed. I rushed to
pick her up and panicked when I saw
her two little teeth covered in blood.

As quickly as I could, I brought her home,
where I woke Mama to show her what happened.
Anger flashed in Mama's eyes.
Katie continued to cry until Mama calmed her

with a bottle of sugar water.
As I climbed on my bed to read
my movie star magazines,
I knew I was in trouble.

After Mama calmed Katie,
she came into my room and
announced my punishment.
"You are on restriction!
No more church for a month.
None. Maybe now you will see how
important it is to take better care
of your baby sister."

No discussion.
Case closed.

Charleston, South Carolina, 1957
The Long Way Home

Now and then I walked through
the antique stores on King Street
on my way home from school—
looking at the chandeliers, china, and silver,
making sure not to touch.

Passing the hotels on Meeting Street,
I watched the bellboys
carry the luggage of well-dressed tourists,
and I wondered where they were going next.

I perused the brochures at the travel bureaus
on Broad Street, and asked for samples
for my geography project about Canada.

I passed the Gullah ladies
by the post office building,
weaving intricate designs
in their sweetgrass baskets
to sell to passersby.

I bought a cherry Coke
at the Rexall Drugstore on Broad Street
and checked out the magazine rack,
browsing through the latest copies
of *Song Hits* and *Hit Parader.*

I crisscrossed down the cobblestone alley,
peeking over walls and garden gates
at miniature statues and fountains
that gurgled and spouted.

I sauntered past the pastel colored
Rainbow Row houses on East Bay Street
with their overflowing flower baskets
and window boxes
before skipping up the steps to the Battery
beside the Charleston Yacht Club
where I watched the sailboats floating across the water
and into my view of Fort Sumter.

I saw my house on Atlantic Street from the Battery,
but continued down East Bay until I reached
White Point Gardens where I stopped
to climb upon a cannon.

I marveled at the Spanish moss on the trees limbs,
and wondered what it would be like to stay
in the Fort Sumter Hotel.

Mr. Wagner waved to me
from his tourist carriage, his horses
clip-clopping along the street.
Walking home down Meeting Street
I admired the lavender wisteria blooming
over the garden walls.

Then I cut through the First Baptist Church
parking lot, ambled down the alley
that connected to Atlantic Street,
and opened the door.

Mama said, "What took you so long?
I'm tired, and I want you to take care of the baby
so I can take a nap."

Charleston, South Carolina, 1957

You Have Chores to Do

Come straight home, you have chores to do.
Quit scribbling in that notebook and get in here.
You should be helping me more.
Now turn down that record player.

Quit scribbling in that notebook and get in here.
Come here and turn up the TV for me.
Now turn down that record player.
The baby's diaper needs changing now.

Come here and turn up the TV for me.
Now go fold that laundry.
The baby's diaper needs changing now.
It's not my job to entertain you.

Now go fold that laundry.
I'm not going to tell you again.
It's not my job to entertain you.
No, you are too young to shave your legs.

I'm not going to tell you again.
You are too old to play with dolls.
No, you are too young to shave your legs.
You'll be the death of me yet.

You are too old to play with dolls.
You should be helping me more.
You'll be the death of me yet.
Come straight home, you have chores to do.

Charleston, South Carolina, 1957
Just Lookin'

My friend, Lee-Lee, and I pedaled the streets
and sidewalks of Charleston
beside Colonial Lake,
past the schoolyard where we played
kickball every day after lunch.
We dropped our bikes at the back door
of Kresge's and rushed
into the store.

Lee-Lee ran, and I chased her
all the way to the front of the store
where we gazed longingly
at the Ponytail Scrapbooks,
touched the cool red leather cover,
and dreamed of buying one.
The salesgirl approached us
in her tight yellow sweater.

"May I help you?"

"No, I said. "We're just lookin'."

Seemed like we were always just lookin'.

Sixth Grade Chorus Concert

We practiced the songs from *Oklahoma*
over and over, and now we were ready.
"Mama, please come to my concert.
Our chorus teacher told us
we were her best class ever,
and even Mrs. Mormon
said so."

But Mama said no.
She couldn't leave the baby.
But she had a surprise for me.
A new dress.

My heart sank
when I saw the pink net formal
"But Mama," I said,
"This is too fancy
for school. It's a prom dress."

"What?!" Mama's eyes narrowed,
"You don't like it? I went all the
way downtown to get this dress for you!
This was an expensive dress!
 I found it on sale.
Just for you!"

"But, Mama—"

"That's ok, Miss Priss," she said.
"If you don't like it,
you don't have to wear it."

"But, Mama—"

"If you don't wear it,
I won't ever buy you anything
again, young lady!
You are just ungrateful!"

Daddy drove me to the school
and dropped me off
in front of the auditorium
where my classmates
entered with their parents.

Backstage, the boys snickered,
"Nice dress."
"Why did you wear that dress?"
the girls asked me.

"Because," I said, "My mama bought it for me."

And I pulled my organza wrap tightly
about my shoulders, hiked up my long
white gloves, and hid the tiny silk purse
that Mama
made
me
carry.

Charleston, South Carolina, 1957

The Picture Show

I stepped up to the ticket booth
at Riviera Theater on King Street,
slid my quarter under the glass,
and entered a world of newsreels,
cartoons, and glamorous movie stars.

From my first-row seat,
I heard the petticoats rustle
across the screen as the 1:15 show began.
My lungs filled with the scent
of magnolia blossoms and wild honeysuckle.
I tramped into the swamps of Raintree County
and viewed the world through
Elizabeth Taylor's violet eyes.

I suffered and became a part of the story,
wearing my character like a long lacy glove,
connecting with the dreamlike movie stars
of my shoebox collection. At the end after
the crescendo, the music ebbed like tidewater,
credits rolled up the screen,
and I read all the names—
as if by some happy accident
I might see my own name climbing the wall.

The audience filed out
into the muggy summer afternoon,
but I remained for the 3:00 p.m. show,
wishing I had money for popcorn or candy.

"Mama won't mind," I told myself.
"I'll clean my room when I get home."
The theater lights dimmed once again.
The film flickered from the tiny window
in the balcony. A teenaged boy stood up
and raised his arms, beams of light cascading
around his body like Jesus
as he cast distorted shadows on the screen.
A bald man across the aisle leaned over
his fat wife to reprimand the boy, but he spilled
his wife's popcorn on the sticky floor,
and her cheeks puffed up like a bullfrog's.
Two red-haired girls in the row behind them
giggled until the usher came to settle everyone down.

On the walk home, I rehearsed
my favorite scenes, mimicked the catch
in Elizabeth Taylor's voice and the cadence
of a Georgia's girl's speech patterns.
I imagined wearing her flowing gowns
and the large straw hats
with ribbons tied under my chin.

I danced along the sidewalks,
skipping over cracks, twirling
my imaginary parasol, balancing myself,
one foot at a time along the curb:
jaywalking, crisscrossing
the narrow streets and alleys,
taking the long way and the shortcuts.

I entered Mr. Anderson's garden.
He waved to me from his veranda.
Holding my shoes under my armpits,
I sat and splashed in his goldfish pond
watching his little concrete fish spout
and gurgle water into the pond.

"Mama won't mind," I told myself.
"I'll clean my room when I get home."

Charleston, South Carolina, 1957

Payback

Approaching the back door,
I heard Perry Como crooning
from the radio about falling stars
and how you should catch one
and hold it in your pocket.
I sang along as I
approached the kitchen.

I smelled the chicken frying,
heard it sizzle in the pan
as I rounded the corner
at the back of the house.
Mama met me at the door
and spat the words at me,
"No more movies or television for a month."
She returned to her frying pan, back turned.
Case closed.

I stroked baby Katie's soft head
with my fingertips. She smiled at me
from her high-chair throne,
her two tiny teeth gleaming like pearls
from her bottom gums.

Tears welled up in my eyes.
"But Mama," I pleaded,
"I am going to clean my room
now that I am home."

She turned to me,
her smile as out of place as
store-bought tomatoes in a summer salad,
"I cleaned your room, Miss Priss."

I ran to my room, fell on my knees,
and searched under my bed.
My shoebox of movie stars
and my Elvis autograph
were gone.

Beneath me, the floor was cool swamp grass.
I cried under the raintree
with a catch in my throat,
while from the kitchen I heard
chicken sizzling and the tapping
of a baby's rattle on her highchair tray.

Charleston, South Carolina, 1958
Mama's Threats

Sunday. Still upset about
my long absence on Saturday:
"You don't do anything to help me!
You can't even take care of the baby!
When you get home from school on Monday,
I am going to put you on a Greyhound bus
and send you to live with your real daddy!"

It was not the first time I had heard this,
but did she really mean it this time?
I had seen John Henry a few times when
I visited my granny, but I didn't really know him.
Would she do that? I didn't want to go.

"I'm sorry, Mama. I'll come home on time
from now on, and I'll keep my room clean."
No answer.
Mama was reading the directions
on the Betty Crocker cake mix box.

My real daddy lived in Georgia. He never
called me on the phone or sent birthday cards.
I really didn't know him. Would she really do this?

"I'm sorry, Mama. I didn't mean to…
I'm so sorry." But Mama did not respond.
Did she really mean it this time?

"Can I set the table for you, Mama?
I promise I will help more, Mama.
I'm so sorry."

No words.

Charleston, South Carolina, 1958
In This House

When I headed out the door
for school Monday morning, Mama
still hadn't spoken to me.

Mrs. Mormon filled the blackboard with
notes from our social studies lesson
for us to copy. The sound of scratching
pencils on notebook paper filled the classroom.

I thought about Mama's anger.
Daddy never yelled at me,
but I knew he could not help.
Once I heard him taking up for me,
and Mama said,
"She is *my* daughter!"

Would she send me away tonight?
Should I tell Lee-Lee goodbye?
That I would not be back to school?
What should I do about my library
book?

Mrs. Mormon erased the board
before I could finish copying
the notes.

Mama did not send me away,
But I worried about it.

After that time, whenever I spoke in a tone
she deemed to be sassy, she said,
"If you get sassy with me again, young lady,
I will give you up to the State.
They will put you in a reform school
for kids who can't mind their parents."

The message was clear:
In this house
children were
not coddled
or cuddled

Mama tallied
misdeeds and careless words
like statistics
on a baseball team,
and she doled out privileges
in meager portions.

I enjoyed Mama's affection
only on the rarest of all occasions
like chocolate covered cherries
on Christmas Day.

Charleston, South Carolina, 1958
The Goodbye Party

Soon baby Jill arrived, and
Mama smiled, saying we were
moving back to Virginia
where her family lived.
Daddy was being transferred
to the naval base in New York City,
 but we would not join him there.

I was leaving my
Charleston friends,
but I knew I would be OK.
We would write letters,
and I would make new friends.
I always did.

But Lee-Lee said I could not go
without a goodbye party.
We took my record player
into the living room,
set out the records,
and waited for the
boys we invited to come
knocking on the door.

When the boys arrived,
Addison, with the pretty
blue eyes, and Marty,
the athlete, we danced and giggled,

enjoying every moment,
until Mama came to the door
of the living room,
and said, "What's happening here?"
"We're having a goodbye
party," I said, "for me."
Mama said, "Well, you can't
have a party without refreshments.
Don't you know anything?"
She sent Daddy to the store
to buy chips and cookies,
and we danced some more—
me with Addison,
Lee-Lee with Marty.

Addison signed my
autograph book:
"Come back to Charleston soon."
I read what he wrote
and smiled.

Portsmouth, Virginia, 1959
Locked Doors

The Navy movers came again,
packed our belongings,
and soon we were
driving back to Virginia.
We traveled this time without
my dog or my fish.
Mama drove us
while I held the new baby,
Jill, and read stories
to three-year-old Katie.

We moved to Academy Park
in Portsmouth,
a housing project built during
World War II to house
the shipyard workers
and Navy families. Aunts and
uncles and a passel of cousins
would keep us company
when Daddy left for the Naval base
in New York City.
We were leaving Charleston
with its gardens, museums,
Spanish moss, cobblestone streets,
and historic mansions,
to move into a tiny house
in a neighborhood
of hundreds of tiny houses, all alike.

Mama finally had her garden
in the backyard,
tomatoes, green peppers, okra, cucumbers,
and even watermelon.

Suffocating from the odors
of green beans and tomatoes
canning on the stove, I wandered
around the neighborhood
on my bike when Mama
locked the screen door
and said, "I don't want you
running in and out!
Go outside and play,
and don't bother me."

Charleston, South Carolina, 1959
From New York to Portsmouth

Daddy regularly phoned us from New York
and Mama's monthly allotment check
paid the bills.

He visited us when he could
and brought gifts from his Navy travels
to Italy, Spain, and Cuba.
Dolls for me.
Jewelry for Mama.

Mama told me to watch
the babies and keep them
quiet during these visits,
mind my manners and
keep my mouth shut.
*Children are to be seen
but not heard.*

"Why, Mama? It's just Daddy."
"Just do what I tell you to do,"
she said.

At breakfast, I picked
up my bacon
with my fingers
and Mama said,
"Use your fork!"
Confused, I looked at Daddy

and then at Mama.
I tried to cut the bacon
with my fork, and it broke
and flipped across the table.

I was shocked when the slap
caught me aside my head.
"Go to your room." Mama said.
I saw the helpless look
on Daddy's face.
"And don't come out
until I tell you."

I lay on my bed and listened
to the sounds of the day
from my room,
the sounds of a family:
Daddy visiting with his babies,
Mama talking on and on about
her garden and her flowers,
and her plans to wallpaper
the living room and paint
the bedrooms.

"You can come out now,"
Mama said.
"Now go and wash those
breakfast dishes."

Portsmouth, Virginia, 1959
Academy Park Neighbors

Mama said she liked our Academy Park
neighbors better than our "snooty rich"
Charleston neighbors.
They were always nice to me.

Ruth from across the street
came knocking on the door

"Can I borrow some sugar so's
I can make some fudge?"

"Sure," Mama said. "Take all you
want. Paulette, get Ruth some sugar.
Sit down and visit a spell, Ruth.
You don't have to rush off."

"OK," said Ruth, "but I can only
stay for a minute. I wanted to thank
you for all you did for my family
while I was in the hospital."

Mama smiled and said, "Oh, it was
nothing. How are you feeling now?"

"Oh, fair to middling," Ruth responded.

As Ruth dropped into the soft sofa
in the living room, I heard them

discussing Ruth's surgery. I filled her
bowl with sugar and brought it back
to her, and then returned to the kitchen.
I was up to my elbows in dishwater
when the phone rang.

Mama yelled, "Paulette, get that telephone!
And I don't want to talk to either one of
my sisters. If it's one of them, tell 'em
I am not home."

"Mama, I don't want to lie," I said, drying
my hands.

"You heard me!" Mama said sharply.

I picked up the receiver of the avocado
green phone on the kitchen wall.
"Hello?"

"Hey, Paulette, is your Mama there?"

"Oh, hi, Aunt Jenny.
She's busy right now.
I'll tell her to call you."

After I hung up, Mama said,
"I told you to tell her I was not at home!"

Ruth lifted herself off the sofa,
picked up her bowl of sugar, and

headed for the door saying,
"I'll see you later.
I'll bring you some fudge."

Mama turned to the kitchen
to deal with me.
"I told you what to say.
You think you are big enough
to stand up to me? You think you
can tell me what you are going to do?"

"No, Mama. I just didn't want to lie.
I just told Aunt Jenny..."

"I know what you told her," Mama interrupted,
"but that's not what I told you to say.
When you finish those dishes, you can just
take these kids outside to play. You are not
going to the pool today."

"But, Mama. You promised if I did the
ironing, I could..."

A knock on the front door interrupted us.

"It's Brenda," I said.

Mama yelled through the screen door,
"Brenda, honey, Paulette cannot come out.
She is on restriction. Maybe one of these days
she will learn to obey me."

Katie and Jill were already in their bathing suits
jumping up and down with excitement.
"Now take them outside!" Mama ordered.

She positioned the window fan in my bedroom
to blow the warm air outside,
and the floor fan in the living room
to blow directly on her. She placed her
rocking chair in front of the TV
and began pasting S & H Green Stamps
in the empty booklets.

Outside Katie and Jill squealed
and ran around in circles
as I squirted them with the cooling mist from the hose.
Brenda walked by with her bathing suit on
and a towel rolled up under her arm.
We waved to each other.
Jill squealed, "Momette! Do it again."
I turned the hose on them again
as they squealed and ran around
giggling on the wet grass.

From my bedroom window, I heard
the voice of the TV announcer,
"Come on down! You're the next contestant
on the *Price is Right*!"

Portsmouth, Virginia, 1959

Seventh Grade

Summer was long and boring.
Some of the neighborhood
girls went to the lake on
the weekends and their parents
offered to take me along,
but Mama would not
let me go.

Most of the neighborhood
girls went to the pool every day
at the recreation center
only two blocks from our house,
but Mama rarely allowed me to go.

I looked forward to attending
seventh grade at my new school.
But after a few weeks
Mama said.
"I want you to stay home
from school this Monday
and take care of the babies.
There's a big sale at
Sears Roebuck.
I'll write you a note."

"I can't do it, Mama,
I have a science test."

Mama said, "It will be OK.
They will let you take a make-up test."

Some of the neighborhood girls
passed our house going to school.
I saw them from the bedroom window
as I changed Jill's diaper.

Portsmouth, Virginia, 1959
Sock Hop

"There's a dance after school, Mama.
It's in the gym, and you wear your socks.
They have really good records
just like the songs on the radio, Mama.
And I want to go."

Mama said, "You know those kids
from Highland Biltmore
think they are better than you?
They may pretend that they
want to be your friends.
But they are looking down
their noses at you the whole time.
They live in their own houses.
Not project houses like ours."

I took a deep breath.
"But I still want to go, Mama."
"OK," she said,
"But don't be bringing
any of them home with you."

At the dance the girls awkwardly
leaned against the wall
waiting for a boy to ask
for a dance.

When they played
"At the Hop,"
girls who could not wait
any longer danced
with each other,
twirling, laughing,
smiling at the boys
who were too shy
to ask a girl to dance.

Portsmouth, VA, 1960

Window Shopping

Mama said I could go to the movies
to see Rock Hudson and Doris Day
with my friend, Brenda.
Walking down High Street
after the movie,
we gazed in the department store
window at the pony-tailed mannequin
posed in a full black skirt decorated
with a pink poodle
tethered on a long leash,
her crinoline slip in miles
of starched pink.

I couldn't wait to be a teenager
and I said so. Brenda said she
was almost thirteen. She would
be a teenager soon and would
wear 100 yards of crinoline slips
and poodle skirts all the time.

I wondered how she would manage
to wear poodle skirts to Catholic school—
but when I asked her,
she paused and then told me
not to worry about it.

I guess she didn't think about that.

Portsmouth, Virginia, 1960

Banana Split

At the lunch counter
in Woolworth's I spent
my last dime on a cherry Coke.
I anchored myself
to the tall stool by
wrapping my feet
around the legs
as I twisted from side to side
and waited.

The waitress arrived with
my drink and Brenda's boat-sized
dish. I sipped on my straw
and savored the syrupy flavor.
In the mirror behind the counter,
I stole glances at Brenda
as she scraped her spoon
across the mounds of chocolate,
strawberry, vanilla.
Holding the cherry up
for me to see, and sucking out
the juice, she pulled the stem
from her lips and chewed slowly,
smiling.

In the mirror I watched
the girl working behind us
at the candy counter.

She had bleached yellow hair
and wore a lavender sweater set,
played with her pop beads,
and smacked her bubblegum
while weighing chocolate malt
balls for a blue-haired lady
in a pink pillbox hat.
In the mirror, I watched Brenda
scrape the last of the banana
from the chocolatey syrup
at the bottom of the dish.
She grabbed her stomach and
said, "I can't eat another bite."

I anticipated her leftovers,
a few bites of vanilla, partially melted
with pineapple topping.
She reached for the salt and pepper
and shook furiously.
She glanced at me and grinned,
and then, as if to remove any doubt,
she leaned over the dish
making guttural animal sounds
and

      spit.

Portsmouth, Virginia, 1960

What You Get Used To

You get used to
     wearing clothes that don't fit,
     last year's styles,
     haircuts-by-mom,
     cheap imitations of what the other kids wear.

You get used to coming home from school to
     babysit
     change diapers,
     fold laundry,
     wash dishes.

You get used to
     making excuses for not doing your homework,
     faking your book report by reading the summary
       on the cover,
     staying home from school to babysit
       when there is a sale at Sears Roebuck,
     C's on your report card.

You get used to
     demands,
     criticism,
     low expectations,
     hurtful words
and you know it won't ever change,
but it will be OK—
     because
     that's what you are used to.

Portsmouth, Virginia, 1960
Eviction

Mama met
the new neighbor
in the backyard,
each of them shaking out
wet diapers and hanging them
on the clothesline.

After that, the young woman
came to our house
several times a day,
wearing her baby on her hip,
her long black, dirty hair
draped down her back.
"Can I borrow your phone?
Do you have any tea?
Could I borrow two pieces
of bread so's I can make a
peanut butter sandwich?"

Sometimes she'd stay a while,
sit and cry, telling Mama
her husband had not found
work since they moved here
from Beckley, West Virginia,
and she was afraid he would
leave her.

After a couple of months,
here she comes saying
"I hate to ask, but could you
lend me twenty cents so's I can catch the bus?"

On the way to school the next day
I saw the legal notice tacked
to her front door
and her whole life in a pile
on the sidewalk:
      a worn-out couch stacked
         with dishes, sheets, and towels,
      a box of Oxydol,
      a jar of peanut butter,
      a bottle of Karo syrup,
      a small electric fan,
      and a photograph
      of her baby in a frame
      flanked by
      two bronze
      baby shoes.

Portsmouth, Virginia, 1960
And Now I Am Thirteen

Locked the bathroom door
took the razor
from the medicine cabinet,
the blade
gleaming,
    gleaming,
        gleaming.

Pulling the blade upward,
beginning at my ankle
all the way up to my panty line
scraping,
    scraping,
        scraping.

Commercials on the television
and Jill
singing,
    singing,
        singing.

On the bathroom door, Katie
knocking,
    knocking,
        knocking.

Mama in the kitchen
calling,
    calling,
        calling.

I knew I was in trouble,
my hand
shaking,
    shaking,
        shaking.

my dry skin
burning,
    burning,
        burning

And then it was done.

I opened the bathroom door
and Katie darted in,
her little legs from the toilet seat
dangling,
    dangling,
        dangling.

In the kitchen,
I washed my hands,
set the dishes
and the silverware
on the table,
poured the sweet tea,

fixed baby, Bobby, a cup of milk,
and settled him in the highchair
holding the cup for him
while he was
drinking,
    drinking,
        drinking.

In front of the television
Jill
singing,
    singing,
        singing.

In the bathroom
Katie
dangling,
    dangling,
        dangling.

In the kitchen,
Mama,
at the stove
stirring,
    mashing,
        frying…
and
under the table, my legs
hiding,
    hiding,
        hiding.

Portsmouth, Virginia, 1960

8th Grade Locker

I went to my locker
after every class
hoping to see Lindsey,
the boy with the locker
next to mine.

Finally,
one day he looked down
at my feet
and said,
"Nice shoes."

Portsmouth, Virginia, 1961
8th Grade Field Trip

"Mama, My class is going on a field trip!
We are going to Washington, D.C.
and staying overnight
in a hotel!"

"We're going to visit the zoo,
and the Washington Monument,
the White House,
and a bunch of museums!
I just have to return
the permission slip now,
and we don't have
to turn in the money yet."

"Hold on Miss Priss."
Mama said,
"You are not going on any
overnight field trip."

"But Mama, puhleesse…"

"I said no, and that's it."

I tucked the permission
slip into my math book
along with my excitement
and closed my bedroom door.

Feeling as out of place
as a parking-lot seagull,
I listened to the girls
at the lunch table
as they talked
about the trip,
planning
what they would wear,
who they would sit with
on the bus,
who they would room with
at the hotel.

On the Friday of the trip
a few of us who came to school
were grouped into a classroom
where we did busy work
all day long.
At lunch time we sat together
in an almost empty
cafeteria.

On Monday,
the field trip kids were
back at school.
The boys laughed about
their water balloon fights
and how Mr. Byrd walked
into the room right at the time

a flying balloon came
in through a window
and bounced on the bed.

They laughed about
how Nat and Ronnie
yelled at girls out the window
from a dark room
while wearing only their underwear,
but Tommy turned on
the light exposing them.

The girls talked about
wearing hats to the cathedral.
Linda hated the
purple pillbox hat her mom
had bought her.

They talked about the long bus ride
and how Paul and Micky
flirted with each other.
Tommy said a girl tried to
put her hand up his sweater
on the bus, but no one
believed him.

Marie came to school
in a cast after breaking her
leg at the zoo.

Everyone talked about
how their feet hurt
from all the walking.

No one talked about
the majestic museums
or the patriotic monuments.

Only Margaret Ann mentioned
the dinosaur bones.

Portsmouth, Virginia, 1961
The Cow Coat

I had just finished folding
the laundry when
Mama entered the house
with several big packages
from her day of shopping.

She pulled clothing
from the bags.
"Look at these cute matching outfits
I found for Katie and Jill."
Red and white candy canes
danced all over the cotton tops.
"Aww…they are cute," I agreed.
Katie and Jill smiled
and rubbed their faces against
the red corduroy pants.

 "Wait until you see what
I bought for you!" She smiled
with wide eyes.
Reaching into a gigantic bag,
she pulled out a coat.
Synthetic fur. White with
big brown splotches.
I wanted to MOO-O-O-O-O.

"Mama—," I hesitated.
"What?" she said.

"Don't you like it?"
I shook my head no.

"I've never seen anything
like this, Mama.
People will laugh at me."

Mama said, "Well, I think it's
cute. Feel how warm it is.
I only paid $15.99 for it.
You could start a new trend."

"No," I said. "I'm not going
to start a trend."

"Try it on," she said. "You don't
know how it will look
until you try it on."

I shook my head.
"I'm not going to try it on.
I'm not going to wear it.
You can just take it back."

"I can't take it back.
All sales were final.
If you don't like it,
I just won't
buy you anything else.
Ever again."

"It's OK, Mama. I will buy
my own clothes."

And I won't be missing school
anymore to babysit while you shop.

Portsmouth, Virginia, 1960

Earning My Way

Mrs. Miller asked me
to babysit on Friday night.
Relieved that I was available,
she told Mama
that she would not trust
most babysitters to handle
her four kids and
her three-month-old baby.
She said to Mama,
"You trained her well."
Mama smiled proudly.

Mr. Miller always
asked, "How much do
we owe you?"
I answered, "Whatever
you want to pay me,"
instead of answering with
the exact amount.
He paid me $5.00 instead
of the $3.50 he owed me
for the seven hours I had been
there.

Mrs. Johnson wanted me to babysit
on Saturday night.
I calculated my pay in my head.
Maybe I would make
enough over the weekend
to buy that blue mohair sweater
I wanted.

Thank You, Mrs. Shaffer

Just suppose
you learned
to read in those
reading circles
in elementary school,
but you never
really loved to
read.

Just suppose you
decided a long
time ago that
reading was
something you did
at school because no
one in your life ever
read a book—
maybe a newspaper,
but never a book.
And you
had no books
at your house,
no bookshelves,
no conversations
about
books.

Just suppose
you faked every
single book
report a teacher
ever asked you
to write by reading
the cover of the book
until you were in
tenth grade and
had a teacher
who would not
allow you to fake it
anymore.

Just suppose
your teacher gave you
a book to read
and you didn't
say no because
your teacher
was so nice and
seemed to care
about you and
you didn't want
to disappoint her.

Just suppose the book
your teacher gave you
was *Frenchman's Creek*
by Daphne du Maurier
and just suppose that

was the first time you
ever read a book from
cover to cover—
and all of a sudden
you could not get enough
of Daphne du Maurier.

Rebecca,
My Cousin Rachel,
Jamaica Inn.

And suddenly the school
library became your favorite
place, and you
wished you had been
one of those children
who climbed a sturdy oak tree
into a spacious tree house
and spent countless hours
under an umbrella
of rustling leaves
devouring
the classics of childhood—
but you knew now
that you have the rest of your life
to read.

Come Straight Home

Come straight home, you have chores to do.
Get your nose outta that book.
You never help me enough. You're just lazy.
Now turn down that radio.

Get your nose outta' that book.
Keep these kids quiet so I can take a nap.
Now turn down that radio.
The baby's diaper needs changing now.

Keep these kids quiet so I can take a nap.
Now go fold that laundry.
The baby's diaper needs changing now.
Take these kids outside to play.

Now go fold that laundry.
I'm not going to tell you again.
Take these kids outside to play.
No, you are too young to go out with boys.

I'm not going to tell you again.
Those dishes aren't going to wash themselves.
No, you are too young to go out with boys.
Take these kids outside to play.

Those dishes aren't going to wash themselves.
You never help me enough. You're just lazy.
Take these kids outside to play.
Come straight home, you have chores to do.

St. Paul's Central High School
Portsmouth, Virginia, 1962
Halloween Dance

Brenda took me to her school
dance at St. Paul's.
Dressed in my costume,
a short skirt,
ponytails tied with
with big red bows,
and a large lollipop
in my hand,
I followed Brenda around
the room as we checked
out the guys who were
standing around
checking out the girls
and their costumes.

I noticed his smile,
he nodded
as we passed.
"Who's that?" I asked.
"Oh, him? That's Roger,"
Brenda said.

At school he asked her,
"Who was that you were
with at the dance?"
"Oh, her? That was
Paulette," Brenda said.

Roger called me on the phone.
I stood in the doorway
of the kitchen, getting
to know him on that
avocado-green wall phone.
He was not discouraged by
kids squabbling in the
background, babies
crying while we talked.
(Kimberly was a newborn
just home from the hospital.)
He understood when
I told him about
Mama's rules:

> Ten minutes on the phone.
> *No more.*
> One phone call each night.
> *No more.*
> One date each week.
> *No more.*
> And my 11 o'clock curfew.
> *Not a minute more.*

Soon we were going to
basketball games,
dances, movies.
Together.

Portsmouth, Virginia, 1962

The Report Card

Mama's academic expectations
were set in stone:
Don't bring home anything
below a C or you will be
on restriction for six weeks,
until the next report card.

But Mama didn't understand
about eyes that would not
stop watching fingers
in typing class or the teacher
who said if you look at your
hands, you will get an F.

On the bus ride home from school,
I cried, knowing that six weeks
was such a long time
without talking on the phone,
without watching television,
without listening to the radio,
without going on a date with Roger.

My friend, Brenda,
oh so practical,
helped me change the
F to a B.

Problem solved.

Portsmouth, Virginia, 1963
Cradock High School

11th Grade Homeroom

On the first day of class,
Mr. Westler left our schedules
at home. Chaos ensued.
He couldn't rush home and
retrieve them because he
rode the city bus to school,
unable to afford a car on
his meager teacher's salary.

Stressed-out secretaries
from the office scrambled
around and finally
solved the problem for us,
as Mr. Westler,
unfazed by administrative details,
moved around the room
with a ruler in his right hand
tapping his left hand gently as he
made his point.

His smile, wide and welcoming,
his joking manner,
intrigued those of us who would return
for his class in the afternoon.

Afternoons with Mr. Westler

He pulled down the dark shades
to filter the afternoon sun flooding
our American history class,
but never once did his passion for
teaching dim.

Sleepy after lunch, we slumped in our seats—
our teenaged bodies ripe with odor
after gym classes—
but Mr.Westler,
a want-to-be-lawyer who didn't realize
he was really meant to be a teacher,
pulled the class discussions out of us
as easily as he pulled those dark shades.

He moved around the room,
tall and lanky, in the same dark
coat day after day, skinny tie
around his neck and dark rimmed glasses
perched on his nose.

He put his fists in his armpits
forming wings to flap and make his point
about "Senator (flap flap) You-Know-Who,"
the Byrd Machine in Virginia, and
U. S. politics.

He was challenging us to think
and participate in class discussions.
There was no sleeping in his class
as he asked questions to keep
us engaged, thoughtful.

When he passed out those
mimeographed test pages,
all discussion questions,
we passed them back
to the students behind us,
each one taking the time to
lift the pages to their noses
and breathe in that purple smell,
while he admonished us
to back up our opinions
with evidence, facts.

At the end of the year,
he handed me my schedule.
He made sure I was
in his government class
in senior year.

Perhaps Mr.Westler
saw something in me
he wanted to encourage.

Portsmouth, Virginia, 1963
Cradock High School
The Announcement

After I learned to love reading
I learned to love books.
Instead of sitting in study hall,
passing notes to my girlfriends,
I worked as a library assistant,
looking forward to the pleasure
of shelving books at the end
of each school day:
content with the order
of library business,
the stability of the
Dewey Decimal system,
a place for everything,
and everything in its place,
the smell of the books,
running my fingers along
the bindings and the smooth
leather covers.

One Friday in November
at the end of the school day
our principal, Mr. Booker,
announced on the intercom
in a trembling voice
that President Kennedy had
been shot in Dallas and had
been taken to a hospital.

And then the bell rang.
I shelved that last book quickly,
as the halls filled with students,
and slamming lockers, but the usual
after-school banter disappeared
as we all hurried home to find normal.

Portsmouth, Virginia, 1963
The Truth

Mama believed in psychics,
ghosts, and visits by aliens
from outer space
and no one could convince her
to change her mind.

Mama said, "Jeanne Dixon
(the famous psychic) predicted
that this would happen
in the *National Enquirer*."
Mama read the *Enquirer*
every week.

Our family gathered in front
of the television set
all weekend
and watched history unfold
in black-and-white images.
A crying anchorman told
the nation about
the horrible shots.

Later we saw the photos,
a president slumping
in the backseat of a car,
the First Lady scrambling
on the back of the convertible,
people in the streets running

in horror from the parade route,
our new president on an airplane
with his hand held high
standing beside a widow
in a blood splattered suit.

On TV we watched in disbelief
as a man at the police station
was escorted through the crowd
and then shot and killed
on live television, without a jury or a trial.
*Would we ever know
the truth?*

The truth was that
a wife lost her husband,
two children lost a
father, and
a nation lost its
president.

Late Bloomer

I sat in a school counselor's
office at the end of junior year,
I waited,
impressed by the number
of books on Mrs. Pollard's shelves,
surprised at the size
of her tiny office and
messy stacks of papers
filling her desktop
and on the floor
surrounding her chair

Rehearsing in my mind
what I would say:
I wanted to go to college,
but I didn't have the science
or math credits required.
I had chosen typing and
shorthand classes instead.

When I told her,
she wasn't surprised.
"Summer school,"
Mrs. Pollard said,
looking at me over her blue
rimmed glasses. She spoke
with authority as if it was all settled.

"You can take Algebra I
in summer school.
You can take Algebra II next year."

"But my Mama won't let me,"
I said. It was the excuse I had
become accustomed to speaking
in a defeated voice
without even putting up a fight.

"What? What do you *mean*
she won't let you?" Her red
hair bounced as she shook
her head in disbelief.
"You want to go to summer school,
and she won't let you?"

I tried to explain.
"I have to help
in the summer.
There are a lot of kids
in my family."

She picked up the phone
and dialed my mother.
When she hung up,
my mother had agreed.
I could go to summer school
if I paid for it myself and
arranged a ride.

Mrs. Pollard smiled.
"Now let's see what we
can schedule for you next
year in science classes."

She believed I could do it.
And that made all the
difference.

Portsmouth, Virginia, 1964
Cradock High School
Sixties Child

In our senior year,
September danced into our lives
like bobby sox across the shiny gym floor,
and we wondered who would make the
cheerleading squad.
In wrap-around skirts and pin-striped
blouses from J.C. Penney's,
we teased our hair
and checked our lipstick
in the girls' bathroom mirror.
Then we rushed to class
amid the slamming of lockers.
With hands holding our hearts,
we pledged allegiance to our flag
while at night we watched a war
that paraded across our TV screens
in black and white.
We believed in fighting for justice
and a better world,
and we knew it had to begin with us.

Portsmouth, Virginia, 1964
Cradock High School
Senior English

Mrs. Boswell

From the first seat
of the center row,
I watched
Mrs. Boswell
with a literature book
clutched to her heart,
announcing,
"This is a wonderful book
to keep forever
and ever."

Never a hair out of place,
never a wrinkle in her clothing,
standing tall with perfect posture,
mesmerizing us with her
stories, breathing life
into the writers.

Mrs. Boswell transported
me to another place,
another time,
once a day,
every day,
leaving behind
if just for the hour
my teenage angst.

Not just grammar
and literature, but
immersion
into English culture:
Wedgewood china,
Chippendale furniture,
thatched cottages,
and green meadows.

Reading *Sonnets from the Portuguese*,
I strolled the garden path
with Elizabeth Barrett Browning
in my ruffled gauze dress
and my parasol in my hand.
I was there—
in love with Robert Browning,
garden gates,
and poetry.

Mrs. Boswell guided us
from Beowulf to Macbeth
and beyond,
experiencing each genre
through our own writing:
psalms and sonnets,
ballads and blank verse.

Memorizing lines, and
reciting them, wallowing
in the beauty
and the wonder of the language,
learning the power of words,
to soothe or incite.

Discovering
that words, chosen carefully,
inspire dreams.

Portsmouth, Virginia, 1964
Cradock High School
Senior English

A Writer Awakened

With *Gulliver's Travels* came
a challenge to write satire
based on something in our lives,
an easy task after struggling
with my shorthand class;
brief forms stalked
and taunted me like Gulliver's
Lilliputians.

Returning our graded papers,
Mrs. Boswell
held mine until last.

Oh, no!
Don't read it, teacher.
It's really not that good.
Read that paper
the straight-A student wrote.

But she said my name,
and then they were all
looking at me.

Shrinking down in my seat,
my face flaming,
I listened as she read my paper

to the class.
An average student,
exerting average effort,
receiving average grades,
unaccustomed to receiving
attention from teachers,
amazed that a teacher
would read something I wrote
to the whole class.

Did she actually like my paper
and believe it was worth sharing?

Babies and Bills and Academy Park

Alone in my bedroom,
I read the application
several times,
filled the answers
in those little blank spaces,
using my best handwriting,
taking my time,
thinking about the people
who would be reading what I wrote.

What if the college allowed me
to attend?
What if I attended college
and lived at home,
rather than going away
to live in a dorm?
Would I be able to do that
and still work?

I had to work
to pay my tuition
and my room and board
at home. Mama had already
made that clear,
$15 a week,
no free rides.

I signed my mother's name to the application.
All I wanted was a chance to learn,
to find out what else was there.
There had to be more to life than babies
and bills and Academy Park.

I folded the application, licked the envelope,
and said a prayer before dropping it
into the mail slot in the school office, and
heading to class.

Portsmouth, Virginia, 1965
Spring Break

I left home two hours before the appointed
time for my interview.
I climbed aboard the bus to downtown
Portsmouth and after a 30-minute ride,
pulled the cord to signal the bus driver to stop
at the next corner.
Got off the bus and waited
until the Tunnel bus came by
heading to Norfolk by way of the tunnel
under the Elizabeth River.
The Tunnel buses ran frequently,
so not a long wait. I climbed aboard,
paid my fare, and rode to Norfolk
where I left the bus and walked six blocks
to the telephone company office,
filled out my application, and
waited for an interview.
Yes, they needed operators.
Yes, they would hire me
to start training immediately,
even before
I graduated high school.

After graduation, I would ride
two buses every day to work
and two buses back home.

Unless, of course, I worked a split shift,
three hours in the morning and
four more hours at night.

On those occasions Daddy planned
to come to get me, because
it would not be safe
to ride the bus that late at night.
In exchange for working the crazy hours,
I would make $65 a week
when I went to work full time.
Very good pay for a girl. I was told
by the interviewer.

I opened a savings account at the bank
next door to the telephone company.

I would save as much as I could
for tuition in case my college
application was successful.

Until graduation,
I would leave school in the afternoons, and
take two buses to receive my training.

Soon I would be
a long-distance operator.

Portsmouth, Virginia, 1965

Congratulations

Mama handed me a package:
"This came for you
in the mail today
from Georgia."

The scribbled return address,
hard to read, indicated that it was
from John Henry.
Upon ripping away the packaging
I found a Timex watch.

In eighteen years,
never a phone call,
no birthday cards,
no Christmas presents,
And even now...

                          no note.

Portsmouth, Virginia, 1965

Graduation

Maybe it was because
it was hot that night,
and she hated
to be in large crowds.

Maybe it was because
she had nothing to wear
in her closet full of bargains
bought at clearance sales.

Maybe it was because
she thought it might rain
that night, and she didn't
like to drive in the rain.

Maybe it was because
she would have to sit
on the bleachers, and
they were just too hard
on her back.

Maybe it was because
she didn't want to miss
Peyton Place, and she
would have to wait a whole
week to see what happened.

Maybe it was because
I spilled pickle juice
on the kitchen counter
and failed to clean it up
that day, and she told me to
pack my things and leave
after my graduation.

Or maybe
it was because
I was a stark reminder
of the biggest mistake
she ever made—
when she
decided to quit
school and marry John Henry.

Whatever the reason,
Mama did not go
to my graduation, and
I didn't pack up and
leave.

Instead, I came home
at my 11:00 curfew,
and cried myself to sleep
as the light from the black and white
television in the living room
flickered through the
crack under my bedroom door.

Portsmouth, Virginia, 1965
Friday Night Date

As I dressed for my date with Roger,
Mama said,
"Oh, you are going out tonight?
That means you are staying home
tomorrow night? Saturday night?"

"No," I answered.
"I am going out again tomorrow
night."

I saw the surprise on her face as
she thought about what to say.

"I am eighteen. I have graduated from
high school.
I am working and paying
room and board.
I will be working many weekends.
So tonight and tomorrow, I will be
going out, and I will be home
by 11:30."

Then I left the room before
she could answer.

Portsmouth, Virginia, 1965
The Letter

Two weeks after graduation
the letter came in the mail
in an envelope marked
Old Dominion College.

"What's this?" Mama asked
as she handed it to me.

I ripped opened the letter
and read. "Mama, they accepted
me! They accepted me
to go to Old Dominion!"

"What are you talking about? How do you
expect to go to college?" Mama asked.
"I told you. We don't have the money
to pay for college. We have four more
kids to think about."

"I'm going to work, Mama.
I'll save my money this summer."

"Just don't think you are going
to get out of paying me room and
board." Mama said. "I need that
money."

She tapped on the bottom
of her pack of Kools,
withdrew a cigarette,
and struck a match.

Daddy said, "You don't need college.
Girls get married and have babies.
Go get a job at the shipyard.
You'll make good money there."

At the telephone company,
I spoke with my supervisor.
"You have only been here two
months," she said, frowning at me
over her glasses.

"You just finished your training.
We would not have hired you
if we had known you would do this."

 I returned to the switchboard,
watched for a green light to
plug into, so that I could repeat
"Operator," over and over
for the rest of the evening,
my college dreams crushed.

Mama Wanted a House

Mama announced,
"I want a house of my own.
Not a project house.
A real house."

Our Academy Park house
was getting crowded
with the addition of Bobby
and Kimberly, now five kids
in a three-bedroom house.

Mama and Daddy
went looking at houses
all over town.
The problem was always
the same. Not enough money.

Eventually, Mama found a house
that was perfect for our family,
one they could afford,
roomy with a big kitchen
and plenty of bedrooms,
a nice pantry for all
of Mama's canned goods,
a yard for the children
to have a swing set,
a place to run and play,
and a workshop space

in the backyard
for Daddy's projects.
And it was right on the bus line,
which would make it
easy for me going to work.
The only thing holding them
back was $500 for real estate fees.

Mama asked
"Do you still have your
savings account for your
college money?"

"Yes," I said. "I do."

"Could you loan us this
money? We will pay
you back. Every penny."

"OK, Mama."

Afraid to say no,
I went to the bank and
withdrew the money so
Mama could get her house.

Portsmouth, Virginia, 1965

Planning

In my new bedroom upstairs,
away from the others,
I filled my bookshelves
with my books and
my journals
with words.

I bought a dictionary
and a thesaurus.
I collected vocabulary
words in a notebook:
words I found everywhere,
in the newspapers,
in magazines, in novels,
on the TV news.

Maybe I could not go
to college now,
not this year—
but one day I would go,
and I would be
prepared.

Portsmouth, Virginia, 1966

Life Moves On

I moved from my job
as a telephone operator
to a secretarial position.
Mama's loan repayment
boosted my savings account,
and I renamed it
"Wedding Savings."

Roger and I planned a life
together after his graduation
from Danville Technical Institute.
He drove home every weekend,
and we wrote letters
during the week.

I chose my china pattern,
picked out my silver and
agonized over crystal patterns.
I collected sheets,
towels, and washcloths
for my hope chest and
vocabulary words
for my notebooks.

After a job offer for Roger
in Richmond, we looked
for an apartment, bought our
furniture, picked out lamps

for our living room, packed
our pots and pans and
silverware in cardboard boxes.
We loved the idea of having
our own apartment
in a big city, moving
away from Portsmouth
and building a life together.
I shopped for my bridal gown,
chose the bridesmaids' dresses,
accepted offers for bridal showers,
and wrote my thank you notes.

I avoided the daily chaos
and drama that enveloped
my life with Mama.

Portsmouth, Virginia, 1966

Opposition

"You can't get married
unless I sign for you.
You are not twenty-one
And I won't do it."

Mama tapped her
cigarette ashes
in the shiny metal ashtray
beside her rocking chair.
"You will be making
a big mistake."

Daddy spoke up
from the kitchen
where he was washing
dishes.

"You will be back
on the doorstep
in two weeks."

I ignored them both,
announced my engagement
in the newspaper,
bought my bridal gown ,
ordered my flowers,
and addressed the invitations,
all with the help of Roger's mother.

Weeks passed until finally
Mama said,
"OK, I'll sign the papers.
I just want you to be happy."

And wouldn't it be nice for you
to have that extra bedroom?

But Daddy said,
"No. I will not
walk you down
the aisle."

"You'll be back
on the doorstep in two weeks."

Then Daddy walked over
and turned up the volume on
the television.
The Lawrence Welk Show
was just getting started.

Portsmouth, Virginia, 1966
Don't Even Try It

Don't tell me
I should not get married
because it didn't work for you…
twice.

Don't tell me
that I should not marry
a Catholic when you
don't even attend church.

Don't tell me
that you didn't love my daddy,
that I exist only because
you were raped by him.

Don't tell me
that you went back to him
each time
because of me.

Don't tell me…

I am not a character
in one of your Bette Davis
movies.

Portsmouth, Virginia, 1966
What I Knew

I knew how to recite
the Prologue to the
Canterbury Tales
in Middle English.
I knew the names
of many trees
by the shapes
of their leaves.
I knew how
to diagram a sentence
with a predicate nominative.
And I knew I had to get away
from Portsmouth.

Far away.

Portsmouth, Virginia
January 14, 1967

Wedding Day

On a rainy Saturday,
Daddy drove me
to the church.
Mama met me at the door
in her navy blue
maternity dress.
She sat in the front row
with Katie, Jill, Bobby,
and Kimberly.

I walked down the aisle
at Holy Angels Catholic Church
on the arm of Roger's Uncle Teddy,
who had no daughters
and was honored
to walk with me.

That day Roger
and I began our life together
leaving behind our families.
We loved them, but
we would make it
on our own.

We didn't need
their advice.

We didn't need
their money.

We didn't need
their signatures
when we bought
our first car.

A new city,
new jobs for both of us.
A new life.

It was a rainy day when we
got married,
but there would be sunshine
and rainbows ahead.

Washington, DC
Richmond, Virginia, 1967

Honeymoon in D.C.

Trampling through
snow-covered streets,
holding hands as we
visited museums
and toured the White House.
We drove through Georgetown
to gawk at the hippies,
snapping photos at Arlington Cemetery,
attending mass at the National Cathedral
in awe of so much beauty in one place,
cramming in as much as we could in a few days.
It felt like one long date—
and then we climbed the stairs
to our third floor-apartment in Richmond,
unpacked our dishes and linens
and began
our new life.

Richmond, VA, 1967
Our First Year

We slept with the windows
wide open in January
as the heat radiated up
from the lower floors and baked us.
The trucks on Chamberlayne Avenue
awakened us in the middle of the night,
changing gears outside
our bedroom
window.

Roger worked as a machinist apprentice
making precise parts for cameras,
(It was said one of them later went the moon
with Neil Armstrong.)
Within a week, I was working in an office,
with a view of the state penitentiary
outside my window,
and we spent our evenings
hanging pictures
and polishing our furniture.

We budgeted $15.00 a week
for groceries and planned our
meals carefully.
My first attempts at cooking
were like science experiments.
Once I lit the gas oven and the flames
licked out in a whoosh,

singeing my hair and eyebrows,
and leaving me shaken.

I washed the laundry
in the basement of our
apartment building,
in washing machines
where we paid twenty-five cents to wash
and ten cents to dry.
I ruined several of Roger's
good shirts before I learned
that you didn't include the fabric softener
until time to rinse.

We didn't have a telephone, but
we made weekly phone calls
from a telephone booth
at Azalea Mall
to let our parents know we were OK.

I wore my skirts short
and Roger grew his hair long.
When the summer heat
drove us out of our apartment,
we walked around in the air conditioning
at Azalea Mall and dreamed
of having a color television
someday.

While reading the newspaper and
clipping grocery store coupons,
I saw a section announcing the schedule
for Richmond Professional Institute
evening classes. We managed to squeeze
out the $16 for my first night class.
Finally, I was a college student.

At Christmas, we decorated our small aluminum tree
with ornaments purchased at Woolworth's,
strung blinking lights
around our bedroom window,
placed our little tree on a table
so it could be seen
as we drove up and down
Chamberlayne Avenue
and smiled at what we had created.

Richmond, Virginia, 1969
Baby on Board

Such excitement
when I found out I was
pregnant!

At work, I told my boss
the news and said that
I wanted to keep my job.
I needed my job.

He looked at me skeptically,
and told me about a girl
who had once worked there
when she was pregnant.
He told me that people didn't think
it looked nice to have
a pregnant girl working
in the office.

He had vowed not to employ
pregnant girls anymore—
but he would make an exception for me.
He said, "Just don't get sloppy."

Richmond, Virginia, 1970
College on Hold

Diving into the pure joy
of motherhood,
I didn't take classes while
I was pregnant or when
my baby boy, Chris,
was very young. It was
hard enough being away
from him all day.

The scent of baby powder
filled the house.
Soft cloth diapers, baby
swings, and rubber pacifiers
became our world.
Afraid of sticking the baby
with the diaper pins,
Roger left the diaper changes
to me.

We checked him
in the middle of the night
to be sure he was still
breathing, celebrated
every new expression,
every smile or cooing sound,
every reaction to the world
around him.

But we quickly discovered
how expensive babies were.
Roger worked overtime
whenever he could.

I returned to work when
Chris was only six weeks old
and found the ladies in the
office wearing polyester pants suits,
the newest style.

The boss had relented to their pleas,
and agreed that they could wear them—
but only if their tops
covered their hips.

I rushed home each day
excited to be a mother,
and grieved over the time
I was missing
while I was at work.

I told the babysitter,
if you see him do something
new, don't tell me.
I want to see it for myself.

Richmond, Virginia, 1973
The Color of Love

Three years later
my baby girl, Betsey,
came into the world,
all pink and full of promise.
We dressed her in lacy bonnets
and smocked dresses.

Once again we celebrated
new foods, first steps,
first babbling words,
and added sibling sweetness
to the mix.
I returned to work, heartsick,
to leave my babies
to be raised by a babysitter,
no matter how good she was.

Mama said I should quit my job
and take care of my children
like she did.

She didn't understand
that times had changed,
that it took two salaries
to survive, that I would
never be able to finish
college without working.

I would never get
to be a teacher.
She didn't understand
that Roger was already
working all he could
to support our family.

Daddy said we should
move back to Portsmouth.
Roger could work in the shipyard.
He would make more money there.
But we said no.
We would not move
back to Portsmouth.

Never.

Richmond, Virginia
1975 - 1981
Night School Student

For many years, I rushed
to the babysitter after work,
rushed home to give the babies
quick baths,
pajamas, dinner—
then off to class with armloads
of textbooks and projects.

When I realized I could cram
the last of my requirements
into one school year,
I quit my job—
even though it paid well
and money was short,
even though taking care of two
children, a house, and a husband
was a full-time job.

For the first time,
at the age of thirty-four,
I was a full-time college student.
I had never attended class
in the daylight
or when I was not already
exhausted.
I was amazed at how being
rested and alert

focused my learning.
And when the time came,
instead of attending
my college graduation,
we attended three ball games:
Roger's game as a T-ball coach,
eleven-year-old Chris's Little League game,
and eight-year-old Betsey's softball game.

Because family
comes first.

Richmond, Virginia, 1981

First-Year Teacher

Student teaching had prepared me
for the life I would live
for the next thirty years:
hauling home mountains of
papers each night for grading,
spending summers poring over
my teacher's manuals, planning my lessons
in minute detail.

Finally, I had my own class!
I prepared all summer
for my fifth graders.
I spent the first week of school
in teachers' meetings and
assembling every detail of my classroom.

On the eve of my first day
at school I had my first teacher dream.
I would continue to have
these dreams each year
before that first day of school—
anxiety-induced nightmares
of classroom management problems
and embarrassing interactions with faculty.

The whole family came out
on the porch that first morning
to wave goodbye as I pulled
out of the driveway and drove
into my new life as a teacher.

Richmond, Virginia, 1981
Bad News

On Friday of that first week,
I was called into the principal's office.
"Our enrollment is down,"
    he said.
"You are surplus,"
    he said.
"You have to pack up and leave,"
    he said.
"But don't be sad.
You still have a job."
    At another school.
    Teaching another grade.

Didn't they know how hard I had worked?
How long I had waited?
How many fifth-grade bulletin boards
I had created?

Obediently,
I did as I was told.
I held back my tears
as I told my students.
I had only known them for a week,
but I already loved them.

I packed up,
pulled the posters off the wall,
and reported to my new school
on Monday, to teach
fourth grade students
an entirely different curriculum.

Richmond, Virginia, 1981
New Teacher Blues

Meandering through those
first years of teaching,
sliding and stumbling,
learning my craft and
balancing family time,
I realized
that most people have no
idea how hard it is
to be a good teacher,
what a sacrifice it is for
families of teachers,
or how much can be
accomplished with
so
little
sleep.

Mama certainly never
understood.

"I don't see why you just
don't just go back to your old
job," she said.

Then she added,
"I can't believe it took
you so long to finish
college."

Richmond, Virginia, 1981 - 2001

The Passing Years

Living my own life,
working hard and
taking care of my family,

I found it necessary at times
to ignore Mama's tearful
or angry phone calls
recounting details of
arguments with her sisters,
her neighbors,
or with Daddy, or
her difficulties raising
a house full of teenagers.
These worries I set aside
into a quiet space labeled
"Not My Problem."

There were also months
and sometimes years
of Mama's silence,
but I needed
to live my life
and take care of my family.

My life was in Richmond—
and even though I was only
two hours away,

I might as well have been
living in California.

In spite of many invitations
over forty years, Mama made
only two visits
to Richmond.

Mama's Dream

Mama told me she was having
a recurring dream:

She answered a knock on the door
in the middle of a rainstorm
and there stood a young man.
Well-dressed. Tall and handsome.
He told her that she was his mother.

He told her that he had been adopted.
All these years he wondered why
she didn't want him?
Why did she give him away?

She said,"No, my baby boy died.
He died." And she awoke
crying.

She wondered if it was real.
She never saw that baby boy,
never had the chance to hold him.
Could someone do this to her?

I took the day off from work,
went to the State Health Department
near the Capitol Building
in Richmond. I completed the
form requesting a copy of my baby brother's
birth/death certificate
to ease her mind.
When I showed her the document,
she realized
it was just a dream.

The Busy-ness of Loneliness

After Daddy's death—
and with my
brothers and sisters
grown and moved
away from home—
Mama filled
entire rooms with her
doll collections:
thousands of dolls,
perfect babies
who never talked back,
just sat there looking
pretty as she smiled proudly,
showing them to people
who came to see Onelia's dolls.

She spent her mornings
with her roses and gardenias,
so beautiful they could
have been in a public garden,
filled Mason jars with
cuttings to share with
anyone who came to visit.

In the afternoons
she stood by the white
picket fence
surrounding her property,

handing candy to children
who passed by on the way
home from school.

On Saturday mornings,
she visited yard sales,
collecting more dolls
and fabric scraps for her quilts.
She spent her evenings
watching old movies
on television and
embroidering quilt tops.

Her door was always
open to neighbors, and
Mama was always ready
for a cup of coffee
or a glass of sweet tea
as she savored the latest
neighborhood gossip.

When she could still
drive, neighbors knew
that she would take them
anywhere they needed to go.

You Made It Come True

One Saturday morning
I helped Mama into my Miata,
buckled down the top
and drove off from her house
with her arms high in the air
waving to her neighbors.

"Y-you m-made it come t-true, "
she said in her broken speech,
affected by her latest stroke.

"What, Mama?"

"When you were a little girl
you said, Mama, when I grow up
I'm going buy a car
and take you for a ride."

Then she smiled.
"You made it come true."

That was the sweetest thing
my mother ever said to me.

I like to think about those
Saturday mornings when
I drove from Richmond
and took her to lunch and to shop

at her favorite place, K-Mart.
When walking became too difficult,
I took her for rides in the countryside
to see the green fields,
and I listened to her stories
of growing up in those red clay mill towns
in South Carolina.

But more and more
she told me not to come
on Saturdays.
And when I came anyway,
she refused to talk to me—
going into her bedroom,
pulling the covers up
over her head,
telling me to go back
to Richmond.

After several strokes
Mama was unable
to take care of herself.
Before long
her dolls were sold,
her beautiful roses and
gardenias withered
from lack of care,
and she no longer stood
by the fence in the afternoons.

In 2006, she fell
in the nursing home
and broke her leg.
Shortly after that,
she had a heart attack.
When I received the
phone call, I drove
immediately to the hospital—
but by then, Mama rested
in silence.
My sisters and I gathered
around her bed.

They talked to Mama in
sweet, soft tones.
I watched but found myself
unable to speak those
words of comfort and
encouragement.

*I never had the chance
to talk with Mama again.*

Regrets

I will always yearn
for what could have been,
and will forever be saddened
by the knowledge that
some things that are broken
can never be fixed.

Mama's Lessons

My mother was on her own
the night I was born,
Christmas Eve, 1946.
She had been on her own
most of her life.
During that time,
she learned many lessons.
Mama taught me those
lessons over the years.

She taught me to love
all kinds of music, old movies,
fried foods, and tacky
Christmas decorations.
She taught me to appreciate
two major food groups
that the government forgot about:
grits and chocolate.

Mama, a woman ahead of her time
in matters of hoarding,
taught me to be a packrat.
Because "you never know
when you might need it"
or "it may be a collector's item one day."

She taught me to be responsible
for my own happiness when she said,
"It's not my job to entertain you.
Now go outside and play."

But Mama also taught me to speak up
for what I believed in,
to work hard for the things I wanted in life,
and to stand tall and salute our country's flag,

She taught me to save for what I wanted
when she put my school dresses
on layaway each summer.
Then she scrimped and saved
from her two jobs,
to pay for them by September
so that I could look my best.

She taught me to offer the mailman
a cold drink on a hot day,
to look for a bargain at a yard sale,
to scatter crumbs for the birds
to eat in the winter, and
she taught me
to root gardenias
by breaking them off
in just the right places.

Perhaps the greatest lesson
she taught me was that
none of us is perfect.

We make mistakes, and we do
the best we can to fix things—
but our children
will always love us
in spite of those mistakes,
because they know
all of us are just learning
how to get along in this world.

We are learning,
every day.

Always learning.

As I gaze into the night sky
I like to imagine Mama filling
hundreds of Mason jars
with bouquets of gardenias,
stringing tacky Christmas lights
on God's pearly gates,
and eating a steak dinner with
Clark Gable.

Book Club Questions and Topics for Discussion

1. Paulette's teachers made such an impression on her that she grew up to be a teacher herself. Think about teachers who influenced you. Who were they? What impact did your teachers have on your life?

2. Paulette's mama was struggling to put together the doll house on Christmas Eve because the tradition in their family was to wake up the children after Santa arrived and allow them to play with their toys for the rest of the night. What unusual traditions did your family have at Christmas or other special holidays?

3. Paulette was expected to assume responsibility for many household duties and care of her siblings during her early years. What family responsibilities did you have during your formative years? How did these responsibilities shape your life?

4. Paulette attended church on her own, visited museums and libraries on her own, rode her bicycle through historic areas in Charleston learning about the town on her own. What effect do you think Charleston had on her life?

5. Family outings were not part of Paulette's experience, apart from Sunday rides in the car. What are the family outings you remember from childhood?

6. Paulette defied her mother when she was thirteen by shaving her legs. In what ways did you defy your parents? At what age?

7. Did you ever express the thought that you would change something from the way you were raised? What changes did you make when raising your own children?

8. The lives of children today are often full of after school activities from athletics, to clubs, to private lessons. Paulette's mama never considered enrolling her in any activities. Can you think of any benefit Paulette gained from that freedom?

9. School and church were definitely an escape from home and huge contributing factors in Paulette's life. What factors influenced your life and made you a better person?

10. The poem at the beginning of the book expresses Paulette's philosophy about children. In what way does this poem speak to you? In what ways can you help children who are not your own although they are in your life?

Acknowledgements

Thanks to all my students in elementary and middle school who laughed with me and shared their writing attempts while I shared mine. I learned so much from you.

Many thanks to my closest friends who encouraged me and believed in me even when I didn't believe in myself: Carolyn Alley, Joan Clarke, Jean Purcell, Karen Maphis, Valerie Bryant, Wanda Kensinger, and Karen Webber.

To my Cradock High School girlfriends who have indulged and supported me over the years, listening to my little poems: Linda Perrot, Gail Novack, Darlene Wylie, Kay Rogers. Linda Rice. And Micky Gastmeyer, who lit a fire under me when she said, "Paulette, would you hurry up and finish writing that book? I want to read it!" Cradock girls really do rock!

Thanks to my very first small writing group. We met weekly and dreamed of making our stories into books. You kept the spark in me alive even when I was too busy with teaching to write: Bonnie Basso and Linda Edlund.

To my writing groups at the Baum Center in Kill Devil Hills, North Carolina and at the Dare County Arts Council in Manteo, North Carolina, especially Michele

Young-Stone. Thank you for sharing your work and helping me grow as a writer until I had a completed work instead of a jumble of random pieces: Martha Pederson Snyder, Debbie Jones Taylor, Wanda Jones, Elizabeth Lindemann, Rebecca Orr, Marion Fritz, Rosemary Rawlins, Paige Kurtz, Marcia Horst, Barbara St.Amand.

To Douglas Scott Jones who read all of my work and whose kind advice helped make this book a reality.

To my Richmond Writing Group friends who encouraged and supported me: Susanna Wilson, Anita Lee, Julie Campbell, Winfree Segal, Lynne Edwards. Your faith in my work kept me focused and determined.

Most of all, thanks to my husband, Roger, who has made me laugh for over 50 years, and whose comment at a poetry reading in Key West many years ago still makes me laugh: *"I thought poetry was supposed to rhyme."* I could not have done this work without your loving support.

About the Author

Paulette Whitehurst was born in Portsmouth, Virginia. She enjoyed a successful career as an educator for more than thirty years in Henrico County, Virginia where she taught elementary, middle school, and community college students and achieved National Board Certification in Early Adolescence/English Language Arts. After retirement, she mentored and coached new teachers and supervised student teachers for Virginia Commonwealth University.

Now living in Chesterfield, Virginia with her husband and her Cavalier King Charles Spaniel, she enjoys reading, writing, and spending time with family.

Paulette is a member of James River Writers, The Hanover Writers' Club, and The Virginia Writers Club.

Follow her on Amazon, Instagram, and her Facebook Page, *Paulette Cawthon Whitehurst, Writer and Educator.* Visit her blog, *From the Fairy Fort*, http://paulette-fromthefairyfort.blogspot.com and her webpage, *Fairyfortbooks.com.*

Made in the USA
Columbia, SC
31 July 2020

15239834R00178